HOLLYWOOD
ON TRIAL

THE 10 WHO WERE INDICTED:

ALVAH BESSIE
HERBERT BIBERMAN
LESTER COLE
EDWARD DMYTRYK
RING LARDNER, JR.
JOHN HOWARD LAWSON
ALBERT MALTZ
SAMUEL ORNITZ
ADRIAN SCOTT
DALTON TRUMBO

HOLLYWOOD ON TRIAL was written by Gordon Kahn in full collaboration with the ten indicted men. All ten assume responsibility for their statements in this book.

HOLLYWOOD ON TRIAL

THE STORY OF THE 10
WHO WERE INDICTED

by GORDON KAHN

Foreword by THOMAS MANN

New York: BONI & GAER

FOREWORD

I HAVE the honor to expose myself as a hostile witness.

I testify that I am very much interested in the moving picture industry and that, since my arrival in the United States nine years ago, I've seen a great many Hollywood films. If Communist propaganda had been smuggled into any of them, it must have been most thoroughly hidden. I, for one, never noticed anything of the sort.

I testify, moreover, that to my mind the ignorant and superstitious persecution of the believers in a political and economic doctrine which is, after all, the creation of great minds and great thinkers—I testify that this persecution is not only degrading for the persecutors themselves but also very harmful to the cultural reputation of this country. As an American citizen of German birth, I finally testify that I am painfully familiar with certain political trends. Spiritual intolerance, political inquisitions, and declining legal security, and all this in the name of an alleged "state of emergency" . . . that is how it started in Germany. What followed was fascism and what followed fascism was war.

THOMAS MANN

In contributing this foreword, Dr. Mann has requested that the Editor explain the earlier use of the text: The words were spoken by him in behalf of the Committee for the First Amendment on the occasion of their nation-wide broadcast during the Washington hearings.

CONTENTS

It behooves every man who values liberty of conscience for himself, to resist invasions of it in the case of others; or their case may, by change of circumstances, become his own. It behooves him, too, in his own case, to give no example of concession, betraying the common right of independent opinion, by answering questions of faith, which the laws have left between God and himself.

THOMAS JEFFERSON to Benjamin Rush

4–21–1803

HOLLYWOOD
ON TRIAL

ATTACK

WHAT were you doing on September 23, 1947?

This is not a trick question. Unless the date has some special significance for you, or calls up some memorable event, you might not remember, except to assume that you were either at work or at home.

Which is where forty-five men and women of Hollywood, California, were on that date. All of them were employed—or between periods of employment, depending on their crafts—in the motion picture industry.

The doors in the homes of these people opened many times that day, for tradesmen and for friends. Then once more—to admit a United States deputy marshal who bore a paper in his hand. A bright pink subpoena, so folded as to show: "By Authority of the House of Representatives of the Congress of the United States of America."

The subpoena commanded each of them to *"appear before the Un-American Activities Committee . . . in their chamber in the City of Washington . . . and there testify touching matters of inquiry committed to the said Committee . . . and not to depart without leave of said Committee. Herein fail not . . ."*

The signature on it was: J. Parnell Thomas, Chairman.

Official—impressive—and to a degree terrifying.

(Suppose it was not Hollywood, but Buffalo or St. Louis and the subpoena came to you?)

It was a command to perform—perform before a legislative ringmaster at a grand, three-ring investigation of Hollywood. Hollywood, to which 85,000,000 Americans in the year 1946 paid an ungrudging box-office tribute of almost two billion dollars.

What was the purpose of the investigation?

In the words of J. Parnell Thomas it was to reveal subversive, Communist, and un-American influence in motion pictures. This leads naturally to the presumption that influences such as that were already *in* the films.

Let us, who make the moving pictures, ask a question of you,

[1]

a movie-goer: Will you name ten films that you have seen this year—or the last—or in the past three years—that were Communist-influenced or subversive of American ideals?

Can you name *one?*

Nothing to be ashamed of if you can't. No such films have ever been made in Hollywood. At one time Mr. Thomas' Committee thought they detected a few and contrived at an elaborate leak. They got as far as *Best Years of Our Lives* and *Margie* before they were laughed right out of the headlines.

Once the keystone, that films are subversive—finds no support in fact, why an investigation of motion pictures at all?

The truth is that they weren't investigating films but men. Not just any men, but nineteen particular men. And it wasn't even on the basis of the films they had written, directed, produced, or acted in. It was their private lives.

These men had been publicly accused by the Thomas Committee of being agents of un-American propaganda in the motion picture industry. And here are the films which only partially represent their work.

Crossfire, Body and Soul, Thirty Seconds Over Tokyo, Hitler's Children, Our Vines Have Tender Grapes, Murder My Sweet, Action in the North Atlantic, Woman of the Year, Objective Burma, Pride of the Marines, Romance of Rosy Ridge, Destination Tokyo, Cloak and Dagger, The Very Thought of You, Tomorrow the World!, Mr. Winkle Goes to War, Sahara, Kitty Foyle, So Well Remembered, Yank on the Burma Road, Rachel.

The fact that these were among the best films ever produced in Hollywood, the most patriotic and among the most successful artistically and financially, impressed the Thomas Committee not at all. They demanded at the hearings in Washington that the men responsible for these films must be driven out of the industry and never again allowed to work in pictures.

And now that has happened. Ten of the nineteen men have been officially blacklisted. Against many screen artists the studio gates are barred.

Squirm as it might, the motion picture industry is today in the tight grip of the Thomas Committee. This is the first medium of communication which the Committee attacked and found it the weakest and most vulnerable. With this scalp at its belt the Committee has announced that it plans to investigate— a polite word—books, plays, radio, magazines—an elaborate eight-point program including labor and education.

We, in Hollywood, who make the motion pictures have seen actual, on-the-ground results of the type of investigation conducted by the Thomas Committee. Films that were ready to be produced have been cautiously laid away on the shelf for another time.

Writers who wrote well because they wrote honestly are hagridden by fears that Thomas won't like this idea or that theme. Producers don't know what books or stories to buy.

Everybody is afraid of being investigated.

The prospects are that pictures like *Grapes of Wrath, Gentleman's Agreement* and others with force and meaning—the kind in which writers, actors, and directors can take pride—will be strangers to the screen of America.

And the film-going multitude will begin to ask itself, "I wonder what's happened to the movies? There was a time . . ."

CHAPTER 1

"The Committee is determined that the hear-
ings shall be fair and impartial."

ON Saturday morning, October 18, 1947, in the Caucus Room of
the Old House Office Building in Washington, D.C., a battery
of nine newsreel cameras stood leg to leg, their cold eyes fixed
on the rostrum. An orchard of powerful photographic lights
blazed. Even in the great crystal chandelier bulbs of high in-
tensity had been substituted for the ordinary globes. The il-
lumination was sharp and shadowless as that of an operating
theater.

A signal was given. A door behind the rostrum opened and
a short, red-faced man strode out with an air of having done
this many times before. His head was almost a perfect sphere,
fringed with sparse gray hair. The features, the hands, the feet,
were small, and his general appearance could be described as
natty—a term he himself would prefer.

His name—J. Parnell Thomas, born John P. Feeney, Republican Representative from New Jersey and Chairman of the
Committee on Un-American Activities of the House of Representatives.

When he was motioned to the chair he was to occupy, the
cameramen saw that there was not enough of J. Parnell Thomas
showing above the tribune. He needed more eminence. They
slipped a red silk pillow under his flanks and a District of Columbia telephone directory under that before he was elevated
to the correct, photogenic height. He was instructed to rise and
make his entrance once more. He complied. Then, with a tape
they measured the distance from his nose to the cameras. "Thank
you, Congressman. That's fine."

J. Parnell Thomas had passed his screen test.

In forty-eight hours the Committee on Un-American Activities of the House of Representatives was to begin hearings on, in their language, "alleged subversive influence in motion pictures."

That day, and throughout the night, every plane which touched Washington National Airport brought newspapermen, magazine writers, radio commentators, and the journalistic aristocracy who analyze each throe of American political life for the millions. Lights burned late in the Washington news bureaus. Overnight-stories and "think pieces" were being written, alerting the nation to one of the major domestic political events of the decade.

The city of Washington wore a tense air, like that on the eve of a coronation—or an important hanging.

And on the night of October 19, 1947, a group of nineteen men—twelve screenwriters, five directors, a producer, and an actor—sat in an apartment in the Shoreham Hotel awaiting word of a conference in progress elsewhere in the same building.

The conferees were the attorneys for these nineteen men who by definition of the Un-American Activities Committee were the "unfriendly" witnesses, and the representatives of the motion picture industry. Their names are important since most of them have principal parts in this chronicle. They are, for the nineteen witnesses, Robert W. Kenny, Bartley C. Crum, Ben Margolis, Charles J. Katz, Martin Popper, and Samuel Rosenwein. Their opposite numbers, representing producers and studio interests, were Eric Johnston, President of the Motion Picture Association of America, Paul V. McNutt, and Maurice Benjamin, attorneys.

The producers' representatives were shown copies of the memorandum filed by the attorneys for the nineteen in which the authority of the Un-American Activities Committee to issue subpoenas was challenged.

"We are maintaining," said Mr. Kenny, "that the Thomas Committee aims at censorship of the screen by intimidation. This accusation is not merely rumor. There is ample reason for this in the public statements of its chairman."

Mr. Johnston replied, "We share your feelings, gentlemen. And we support your position."

Doubtless, the advocates of Jack L. Warner, Vice-President of Warner Brothers Studio, were privy to the testimony which their client had given at the not-so-secret investigation by J. Parnell Thomas in Los Angeles five months earlier. Testimony, incidentally, which was to be painfully recalled to Mr. Warner the following day.

Mr. Kenny then remarked, "The subject with which we are chiefly concerned is the character of the statements attributed to J. Parnell Thomas by the newspapers. He was quoted as saying that the producers had agreed to establish a blacklist throughout the motion picture industry."

Indignantly, Eric Johnston answered, "That report is nonsense! As long as I live I will never be a party to anything as un-American as a blacklist, and any statement purporting to quote me as agreeing to a blacklist is a libel upon me as a good American."

Mr. Crum rose to shake Mr. Johnston's hand, saying, "Eric, I knew you were being misquoted. I'd never believe that you'd go along with anything as vicious as a blacklist in a democracy."

"The witnesses we represent," Mr. Katz added, "will be more than delighted to have that assurance from you."

"Tell the boys not to worry," Johnston concluded. "There'll never be a blacklist. We're not going to go totalitarian to please this committee."

The nineteen "unfriendly" witnesses received this report from their attorneys with audible cheers. None doubted that the producers' representatives recognized the Thomas Committee as the common foe of the men who produced America's motion pictures and of the artists who conceived them.

Tomorrow the hearings would begin. The producers, as announced by the Committee, would be the first to take the witness stand, and the defense of the American screen was in good hands.

At nine o'clock on the morning of October 20 there was already a long line of spectators in the rotunda on the second floor of the House Office Building, waiting to be admitted. An hour later it was thronged with people crowding toward the doors of the Caucus Room. The majority of them were men and women well beyond middle age. They could not be called simply idlers, and one newspaperman characterized them as mostly "pensioners" for whom the daylight hours drag.

J. Parnell Thomas entered the already crowded Caucus Room at twenty minutes past ten o'clock. He nodded to several people here and there without deviating from the bee line to his chair behind the rostrum. Other members of his committee who had already taken their seats were John McDowell of Pennsylvania, Richard B. Vail of Illinois, and Richard M. Nixon of California.

The newsreel cameras, their motors murmuring, caught J. Parnell Thomas as he entered. The flashlight bulbs of thirty news cameramen volleyed silently in his face until he waved his small white hand for a halt.

There was a long silence as J. Parnell Thomas seated himself and surveyed the vast room. The first object of his satisfied gaze were the press tables accommodating ninety-four newspapermen and women that first day. About one-third of the right side of the room, through which the eastern sun slanted, were rows of control panels and other broadcasting equipment manned by technicians and announcers. Loudspeakers for the public address system which amplified every whisper in the hearing room were clustered strategically around the walls. Three microphones were on the rostrum, additional ones on the table at which the witnesses were to sit, and several more in front of Robert E. Stripling, chief investigator for the Committee.

As he contemplated all this—and found it good—J. Parnell Thomas failed to note the absence of something which *should* have been there. Something which is present in every forum and legislative hall throughout the land. At every civic process, from the recording of a deed to a hearing of the Supreme Court. But not here.

Nor did J. Parnell or any of the hundred newspapers covering the hearings ever mention the fact that nowhere in that room was there an American flag.

The calmest man in the room was Robert E. Stripling, a tall, wan Southerner who had climbed from clerk of the Dies Committee, a precursor of the present tribunal, to chief investigator.

He was in temperament everything that his superior, Thomas, was not. When, as crises developed, Thomas' face reddened, the investigator's face grew slightly paler.

For the ten days of the Hollywood hearings, J. Parnell Thomas wielded the gavel. But the whip hand was Stripling's. There was a sound like the whispering of leaves as clerks for the Committee handed around to the press the prepared opening statement of the chairman.

The radio switches were opened . . . "Testing . . . testing . . . one—two—three—four . . ." Announcers, their lips close to their microphones, were describing the scene to their listeners or recording their observations for later broadcast.

"The Committee is determined that the hearings shall be fair and impartial," Thomas read from his prepared statement. "All we are after are the facts."

CHAPTER 2

"Do you wish me to answer that as a motion picture executive or as an American citizen?"

IN the motion picture industry the president of a producing company is virtually anonymous; whereas the individual who wields the greatest power is usually called Vice-President-in-Charge-of-Production. That is the title held by Jack L. Warner in the vast studio which bears his name and where he makes full use of the authority vested in him. He uses it oftener and more vigorously than any of his rival vice-presidents-in-charge-of-production in Hollywood.

J. L.'s frown can nip the career of an actor, writer, or director in the bud, or any time after it has flowered. A stroke of his pen can reduce (and has) the Warner Brothers' studio payroll twenty percent or more. He is shrewd. In small matters as well as large. Many Warner employees treasure the telegraphed Christmas greetings signed "Jack and Ann Warner, Cannes, France," but which were dispatched more economically from a Hollywood Western Union office.

At his studio clock-punching is a ritual. Even executives, members of the talent ranks and others without time cards are under rigid surveillance of the studio hours they keep. The commissaries at most of the other studios serve three meals a day. Warner's, only one. No dawdling is the policy here.

The Warner Brothers Office of Plant Personnel is something more than a headquarters of the studio police and other maintenance employees. It is, instead, operated along the lines of the Federal Bureau of Investigation. Its chief is F. Blayney Matthews, a former investigator for the Los Angeles District Attorney's office and who still retains important "connections."

Warner himself takes credit for devising an employment application and personnel record which all of his employees are required to fill out. One question on it demands:

Are you a member of any organization, society, group or sect owing allegiance to a foreign government or rule? (*Yes or No.*)

Other questions pertain to the employee's religion, lodge, or club affiliations and ask for details concerning amounts of insurance carried and the ownership of real property. Not without pride Warner commented on this questionnaire before the Committee, "We had plenty of rebuffs from people who had to answer them or they wouldn't get a job."

He has amassed (by his own figures) a personal fortune of $40,000,000.

For almost twenty years, the Warner Brothers studio enjoyed the public esteem. It pioneered in sound pictures and thence onward in the production of musical films. Its era of greatest achievement was the period when it produced films that almost kept abreast of the headlines. It sought and developed new stars, directors, and production techniques.

Due to the character of its productions, scoffed at by the more lagging companies as "message pictures," the Warner company achieved a reputation as a public-spirited concern within the industry as well as outside. However, in the Fall of 1945 a serious labor situation prevailed. Strikes developed. On the morning of October 5 of that year, a picket line of more than a thousand formed in front of the Warner studio gates in Burbank.

Events that day took a serious turn. Warner issued an ultimatum to the strikers to disperse. Instead, their numbers grew. Then, shortly before noon tear gas bombs were hurled from within the studio gates. More followed. The picketers ran. But later their lines reformed. The Warner Brothers fire department coupled their hoses and turned the powerful stream on those demonstrating outside. Men and women were flung to the ground by the high pressure jets and swept along like chips. A score were injured. Warner sent for police reserves who brought up tear gas guns and began clubbing people off the streets of Burbank.

In that one day, the Warner Brothers under J. L. Warner, Vice-President-in-Charge-of-Production, declined noticeably in public relations. Publicly and privately J. L. Warner declared that he was through making motion pictures about "the little man." It can be said that he has kept his word.

It is well known in the motion picture industry that J. L. Warner enjoys public speaking. He has appeared from time to time before industry and civic groups, always accompanied by his personal publicity staff and a platoon of photographers from his own studio. It is also noted that he has a habit of abandoning the text of his prepared speeches and indulging in long, extemporaneous asides. On one occasion, when he returned from a junket to Europe conducted for motion picture magnates by the State Department, he decreed an audience at the studio and spoke uninterruptedly for three hours and twenty minutes —on his employees' time, after studio hours.

This penchant for talking made Warner a windy and cheerful witness at the preliminary hearings of the Thomas Committee in May. The object of the probers at that time was to interview the "friendly" folk in the motion picture industry and wheedle out of them the names of the "unfriendly" elements. Warner needed no cajoling. He turned the affair into a gabfest.

Words gushed from him in a torrent. And when words failed him, which was rare, he served up reams of printed matter, all attesting to the eminence of the Warner Brothers. In all, he fattened the record by approximately 57,000 words, a high for the hearings. He sang loud and lustily.

"I can look in a mirror," he said, "and see three faces."

Whereupon one newspaperman was moved to comment, "And why shoot them all off at once?"

It was Warner's opinion that screen writers were the principal offenders in the black arts of "injecting Communist propaganda" or as he occasionally called it, "stuff" into films. He then proceeded to tell the Committee how he got rid of the "subversive" writers even *before* they were able to get away with a single line of propaganda.

(Wherever, as will soon be obvious, errors of grammar appear in the quoted remarks of Mr. Warner, as well as that of other witnesses, the reader is assured that they are not typographical errors. The statements are in context, and *verbatim*—as they were uttered and printed in the official record.—*Editor*)

MR. WARNER: Anyone whom I thought was a Communist, or read in the papers that he was, I dismissed at the expiration of his contract. In one fellow's case I had to hold onto him because we were dropping them too rapidly and it was too apparent.

MR. STRIPLING: Why did you say it was too apparent?

MR. WARNER: By letting them all go at once, in one day.

He admitted that when he called people Communists "it was from hearsay." He relied for those matters on the *Hollywood Reporter,* a daily film paper published by W. R. Wilkerson, a restaurant and resort proprietor.

But of six writers he was certain.

MR. STRIPLING: And you let these six people go. Can you name the six?

Warner did better than that. He named sixteen.

The first one is Alvah Bessie. Then Gordon Kahn . . .

At that point he stopped to make a few animadversions on the character of Kahn, and to regale the Committee with a chatty account of how he tried to suppress a magazine article which Kahn had been assigned to write in Mexico.

I gave instruction all along the line not to have him in there, but he gets in. The day I let him go he was on the plane for Mexico. He was writing a story for *Holiday* magazine, one of the Curtis Publishing Co.'s magazines. I tried through the New York office to tell them the fellow was "off the beam" and should not accept his material.

I was told, "You are not going to interfere with the right of free speech and freedom of the press." I got the usual run-down of a publisher. That is what they told my man. I tried to have the story stopped for this particular paper, but he is writing it. In fact, we were chastised for interfering with their business, so I got off of that.

Warner had evidently been chastised by Johnston and Mc-Nutt as well for having the temerity to instruct one of the biggest publishing houses in the world what to print. This was the first of his testimony that was spoon-fed back to him so that he could retract and apologize, or both. On October 20, he tried:

I meant this: That the Curtis Publishing Co., by refusing—at least to anybody in our company—to publish this Gordon Kahn's article, good or bad, whatever it was, I don't know, proves decisively that the American way of life, free speech and free press, is very, very important to retain and never let it go. . . .

Therefore, I believe—I pay my deep respects to the Curtis Publishing Co. for their American stand on free press and free speech.

Warner was slightly in error. The Curtis Publishing Company did not refuse to publish the article. It was duly printed in the January 1948 issue of *Holiday* magazine. In addition there was an editorial note in the same issue describing it as the article which Warner attempted to suppress.

But back to the names of the writers he had "let go." . . .

Guy Endore, Howard Koch, Ring Lardner, Jr., Emmet Lavery . . .

That group, with Alvah Bessie and Gordon Kahn, made six. But Warner bowled right along. . . .

. . . John Howard Lawson, Albert Maltz, Robert Rossen, Irwin Shaw, Dalton Trumbo, John Wexley. You know these names.

Mr. Thomas: That is a very familiar list.

Mr. Warner: Julius and Philip Epstein, twins.

Mr. Thomas: What are they doing?

Mr. Warner: They are at M.G.M. I will give you my theory of what happened to these fellows when I finish. . . . Sheridan Gibney, Clifford Odets. That is all of my list.

That, in fact, was too many. Had he taken the trouble to consult his records, Mr. Warner would not have had to go over the ground again and remove a few names from his "bad" list. Again in October, J. Parnell Thomas helped him out of the trouble he had gotten into in May.

Mr. Thomas: On all those other names you would make the same statement in relation to them today as you did on May 15?

Mr. Warner: I would with the exception that I have looked up one or two of the men; it has been so far back. I was naturally carried away at the time with this testimony being taken. I was rather emotional, being in a very emotional business, to a degree. There are several names here, one or two that I have mentioned that I haven't any recollection of at this time, after careful investigation, having written any subversive elements.

Mr. Thomas: You better name them.

Warner then proceeded to clear those writers who, in his words, "have not attacked the Government with violence and overthrowing":

"Guy Endore—it has been so long ago."

"Sheridan Gibney." For no particular reason.

"Julius and Philip Epstein—they were always on very good American films and there is very little can be said about them," except: "As I said, they do it in a very joking way. The rich man is always the villain, which is as old as the world itself."

The members of the Committee craned forward. They were about to hear one of the nation's most prosperous motion picture magnates discuss economics.

Ever since one man had $1 and the other fellow had another dollar there has always been that envy between man and man.

Mr. Thomas: Don't you think it would be very foolish for a Communist or a Communist sympathizer to attempt to write a script advocating the overthrow of the Government by force or violence?

Mr. Warner: Do you wish me to answer that as a motion picture executive or as an American citizen?

J. Parnell Thomas' reply was as courtly as anything to be found in *Idylls of the King*.

Either one, it makes no difference. You are both.

Hollywood was puzzled when J. L. Warner did not correct his earlier list of offending writers to absolve Howard Koch. The film colony is familiar with the facts concerning Koch's departure from the Warner studio. He had been one of its most valuable writers and his contract had a year or thereabouts to run in October 1945. This was the time, it will be recalled, when the bomb-hurling took place in Burbank. Koch protested the participation of his employers in that act and demanded his release from the contract. The studio was willing if Koch would pay them $35,000. Koch regarded this an unconscionable sum and offered them $10,000. The studio accepted and Koch went to work elsewhere.

In identifying the other former Warner Bros. writers, the Vice-President-in-Charge-of-Production was asked by Stripling:

"Could you give us the names of some of the pictures in which they injected their lines or propaganda?"

Warner did not fall for that one. Not too hard, at any rate. He corrected Stripling. "They endeavor to inject it. Whatever I could do about it—I took out."

MR. STRIPLING: Identify the films.
MR. WARNER: Alvah Bessie, *The Very Thought of You*. Gordon Kahn, *Her Kind of Man*. . . . Howard Koch, *In Our Time*. . . .
As far as Koch is concerned, he was on 20 scripts, but he never got anywhere because he always started out with big messages and I used to take them out. . . .
Ring Lardner, Jr., . . . he didn't put any message in *The Kokomo Kid*. Or Emmet Lavery, he has no credits. We throw his stuff in all the way and pile it up.
John Howard Lawson, *Action in the North Atlantic*.
Albert Maltz in *Pride of the Marines*.

J. Parnell Thomas at this point wanted to know, "Did Maltz get much into *Pride of the Marines?*"
No, by Godfrey, he didn't. But he tried, said Warner, who ran that film himself and detected:

[15]

One little thing where the fellow on the train said, "My name is Jones, so I can't get a job." It was this kid named Diamond, a Jewish boy, in the Marines, a hero at Guadalcanal.

There might have been something there, Warner allowed, but if there was, he didn't recognize it.

Some of these lines have innuendos and double meanings, and things like that, and you have to take 8 or 10 Harvard law courses to find out what they mean.

MR. STRIPLING: They are very subtle.

MR. WARNER: Exceedingly so.

He then cited Robert Rossen for *They Won't Forget* and *Dust Be My Destiny;* Irwin Shaw for *The Hard Way,* and Dalton Trumbo as collaborator with Lardner on *The Kokomo Kid.*

It gives you an idea; they work in pairs.

He credited John Wexley with the script of *City for Conquest* and then reverted to a description of *Action in the North Atlantic,*

. . . which was produced for the merchant marine because at the time they could not get proper enlistments and all that. I made this film. . . . I don't know whether you saw that or not.

MR. STRIPLING: Yes.

MR. WARNER: Naturally John Howard Lawson tried to swing a lot of things in there, but to my knowledge there wasn't anything.

MR. STRIPLING: John Howard Lawson tried to put stuff in?

MR. WARNER: Yes; I would say he did in one form or another.

And the Epstein brothers again. "They did very good work at one time," said Warner, "but they fell off."

"They worked on a picture called *Animal Kingdom,*" he added. "As I recall, that was aimed at the capitalistic system— not exactly, but the rich man is always the villain. Of course, those fellows getting two or three thousand dollars a week aren't rich men. I don't know what you would call them. Both of those fellows work together. They are never separated."

In the same encounter with the Committee, Warner gave his observations also on the vulnerability of the legitimate stage to "stuff."

In New York I saw *All of* (sic) *My Sons,* written by Arthur Miller. . . . That play disgusted me. I almost got into a fist fight in the lobby. I said, "How dare they?" They write about 21 little cylinder heads that were cracked. And the play is a good play, but it has all of this stuff in it. In fact it won the Critics' Award in New York, and was directed by a chap named Elia Kazan who is now at Twentieth Century-Fox as a director. He directed *Boomerang* and is now going somewhere to make a picture for them.

MR. THOMAS: What is the new one?

MR. WARNER: *Gentleman's Agreement.* Can I say something off the record?

MR. THOMAS: Put it on the record.

MR. WARNER: This fellow is also one of the mob. I pass him by but won't talk to him.

Mr. Kazan, who did indeed direct *Gentleman's Agreement,* when informed of J. L. Warner's opinion of him, appeared not distressed.

Altogether, during this part of his Los Angeles testimony, J. L. Warner brought in the names of seven of the nineteen men subpoenaed as "unfriendly" witnesses and incidentally mentioned as their work some of the outstanding motion pictures made at his studio. Four of the seven writers he mentioned as having tried to put "stuff" into pictures were among the ten men indicted for contempt of the Un-American Committee and are, at this writing, standing trial in the Federal Court.

In his eagerness to show the congressional investigators that there was no more alert guardian of the films against "stuff," J. L. Warner also added the name of Clifford Odets and the film *Humoresque.* This was the second filmic version of a novel by Fannie Hurst. He spoke from written memoranda.

John Garfield played the part of the boy and he was mad at Joan Crawford for romantic reasons and said, "Your father is a banker." He was alluding to the fact that she was rich and had all of the money.

[17]

He said, "My father lives over a grocery store." That is very, very subtle, but if you see the film with those lines in it you will see the reason for it. But it is not in the film. I eliminated it from the script. Sometimes you eliminate these things and they leave them in because it plays good and everybody is trying to be a Voltaire. All these writers and actors want to "Voltaire" about freedom of press and freedom of speech.

Thomas' curiosity was not at that moment over Warner's criticism either of films or society. He wanted to know about the film, *Mission to Moscow* . . . a great deal about it. Representative Vail, who was obviously plumping for the blacklist appeared eager to move into that phase.

CHAPTER 3

"I can't for the life of me figure where men could get together and try in any form, shape or manner to deprive a man of a livelihood because of his political beliefs. . . . It would be a conspiracy, the attorney tells me, and I know that myself."

WHOEVER composed the manifesto which J. L. Warner read to the Un-American Activities Committee on the opening day of the Washington hearings did a superb job. It concluded, "There is no positive guide to determine whether or not a person is a Communist; and the laws of the land, which are in the hands of you gentlemen, offer no clean-cut definition on that point."

(That would be attended to later, the Committee informed Warner, by a series of bills determining by congressional fiat that American Communists were agents of a foreign, enemy power.)

His voice becoming oratorically deeper, Warner went on:

"We can't fight dictatorships by borrowing dictatorial methods. Nor can we defend freedom by curtailing liberties, but we can attack with a free press and a free screen. Subversive germs breed in dark corners. Let's get light in those corners."

By allowing Warner to make his preliminary statement without hindrance, the amenities were observed. But the Committee appeared eager to clear away the la-de-da and get down to the real business of the hearings. In a short time, the nature of this real business was exposed.

It was precisely what the attorney for the nineteen "unfriendly" witnesses warned it would be—an attempt to institute a blacklist in the motion picture industry.

This grimly serious matter of blacklist, whenever it had been previously mentioned, was talked about as "strong rumor," and had always been filtered through the press friendly to the idea of a blacklist.

How thoroughly official it was became clear when the May 1947 testimony of J. L. Warner was read into the record of the Washington hearings. It was Stripling who broached that subject:

Don't you think the most effective way of removing these Communist influencers is the pay-roll route? In other words, if the owners and producers cut these people off the pay-roll it would eliminate it much quicker than a congressional committee or crusades or so forth?

Did J. L. Warner sense a trap in that question and parry it politely? He said simply, "Well, that definitely would be. If you drop them out of pictures then the Communists would have other ways of doing it."

In May, neither Stripling nor Thomas was any blunter than that about the blacklist. Whatever questions they asked simply veered on it and tended to get Warner's dander up about the large salaries these "subversive" writers were wresting from one studio or another.

However, on Monday, October 20, the Committee came right out with it. They didn't flatly say "Blacklist 'em!" because blacklist is still a dirty word in every organization of professional men, including writers' guilds, in America. But blacklist is what they meant.

This particular manoeuver of the Thomas Committee had been allotted to Representative Vail of Illinois, who sat on the left hand of J. Parnell Thomas. He took over the questioning of Warner and began, rather slyly, to ask about the aims and purposes of the Motion Picture Association of America to which the major producing companies belonged and which had Eric Johnston as its $100,000-a-year president.

MR. VAIL: In your testimony, you stated certain of your employees were discharged on suspicion, apparently, of being Communists and they were promptly hired by your competitors. Did I understand you correctly?

[20]

Mr. WARNER: Some of them were, yes, sir; that is correct.

Mr. VAIL: What is the purpose of the association? (The Motion Picture Association.)

It was a pretty crude gambit. Warner was prepared for it. He answered manfully that the Association has nothing whatever to do with the hiring or firing or making of any terms of business contracts.

To the 19 "unfriendly" witnesses and their lawyers, this response was most significant. The hitherto "strong rumors" that the Committee was prepared to demand a blacklist became the naked truth. Were Johnston and McNutt aware that this was the time and place to carry out their solemn pledge of the night before that they would fight anything so totalitarian as a blacklist? Did Warner understand this as well as Johnston and McNutt? How would he stand up if the Committee kept hammering?

Vail plunged ahead:

Wouldn't such an association provide a splendid piece of machinery for distribution of information between producers as to the type of individuals that are employed by the industry and who are concerned with subversive activities?

J. L. Warner's answer was heartening. First of all he gave the Motion Picture Association a clean bill of health by declaring that he was rather active in the Association and that such an idea had never been brought up in it, either in writing or by the spoken word. He added, "Of course, I don't believe it would be legal in my opinion—speaking only personally— to have the Association or any men band together to obstruct the employment of any other man. I don't believe the Association would have anything whatsoever to do with that type of operation. I would not be a party to it and neither would any of the other men, from my knowledge of them."

That should have been clear enough to the Committee. But Vail wasn't finished. Although he attempted to frame his next remarks as a question, it was really a suggestion that a blacklist would be perfectly proper.

Mr. VAIL: Since we recognize the fact that motion pictures represent a forceful vehicle for the distribution of subversive information, it would seem to me that would be a very important bit of business for your association. . . .

Mr. WARNER: That sounds rather logical, but it wouldn't hold water. . . . I wouldn't be a party with anyone in an association, especially where you would be liable for having a fellow's livelihood impaired; I wouldn't want to do that.

Mr. VAIL: Would you be deeply interested in providing a livelihood for the individual who was attempting by subversive methods to destroy this form of government?

Warner acted as if this line of questioning was getting tiresome and Vail, for the time being dropped the matter.

Representative John McDowell of Pennsylvania took over. Throughout the hearings it was apparent that McDowell carried the ball for that group in Congress principally interested in outlawing the Communist Party.

Mr. McDOWELL: Just one question, Mr. Warner. . . . You know, of course, this committee has before it a resolution outlawing Communists and also another resolution defining Communists. Would you advocate that the Congress adopt either of these resolutions?

Mr. WARNER: . . . I would advocate it providing it did not take away the rights of a free citizen, a good American to make a livelihood, and also that it would not interfere with the Constitution of the United States as well as the Bill of Rights.

That should have been enough, but the Committee kept boring in. Warner's attitude so far was not limp enough to suit them. He needed a little more pummeling.

Mr. McDOWELL: You know during Hitler's regime they passed a law in Germany outlawing Communism and the Communists went to jail. Would you advocate the same thing here?

That was not very bright of Mr. McDowell and Warner gave him the proper answer, "Everyone in this room and everyone in the world knows the consequences of that type of law."

McDowell seemed displeased. He pouted, "Canada has a similar law; also Panama and many South American countries. Thank you very much."

But J. Parnell Thomas was there in the pinch. Much better at cross-examination than any of his colleagues, he got precisely the answer that McDowell was struggling for.

MR. THOMAS: If we passed a law, that would be proper legal procedure, wouldn't it?

MR. WARNER: I, as an individual citizen, naturally am in favor of anything that is good for Americans.

MR. THOMAS: Are you in favor of outlawing the Communist Party?

MR. WARNER: You mean from the ballot?

MR. THOMAS: Yes, making it an illegal organization.

MR. WARNER: I am in favor of making it an illegal organization.

MR. THOMAS: You are?

MR. WARNER: Yes, sir.

On that subject, J. L. Warner was finally, after some hanging back, on the record. However, the Committee hadn't yet gotten the answer they wanted from him on the subject of the blacklist. There was time. It was eleven-thirty in the morning. They would revert to it again before he was dismissed from the stand. Meanwhile, J. L. Warner had an axe of his own that needed grinding—a little matter of skirt-clearing with respect to the production of *Mission to Moscow*.

For a long time political enemies of Franklin D. Roosevelt gained wide publicity for their charges that the Warner Brothers were "ordered" to make that film. Thomas sought to put proof of this into the record when he questioned Warner in May. It was brought up at the conclusion of Warner's breathless discussion of how patriotically his studio operated during the war.

MR. STRIPLING: Were you asked to make *Mission to Moscow*?

MR. WARNER: I would say we were to a degree. You can put it that way in one form or another.

MR. THOMAS: Who asked you to make *Mission to Moscow*?

MR. WARNER: I would say the former Ambassador Davies.

Warner, further along this line of testimony, appeared to be somewhat uncertain as to "who contacted whom" about the film

[23]

production—whether it was himself, his brother H. S. Warner, or whether Davies made the original contact. However, he recalled that Prof. John Dewey of Columbia University criticized the project severely. But from what he read and heard, Warner explained, "He (Dewey) was a Trotskyite and they were the ones who objected mostly to this film because of Lenin versus Stalin. . . ."

But that wasn't what the Committee was after.

MR. STRIPLING: I will be very frank with you. The charge is often made and many statements have been made to the committee to the effect that *Mission to Moscow* was made at the request of our Government as a so-called appeasement or pap to the Russians; in other words, it was produced at the request of the Government. Now, is such a statement without foundation?

MR. WARNER: I see what you mean. No, it is not without foundation. . . .

That, it is essential to recall, happened in May.

In due course, on October 20, J. L. Warner had those morsels of testimony concerning *Mission to Moscow* served up to him. Stripling read back to him those earlier answers.

MR. WARNER: There is a correction I wish to make. . . . I just wish the record to show that I want to make a correction.

He then declared that when he said that Ambassador Davies asked him to make the picture, he (Warner) was mistaken.

. . . Since making that statement I have gone over the authentic details of what occurred, and here they are in sequence. . . . My brother contacted Mr. Davies after reading *Mission to Moscow* as a best seller on the stands and in the newspapers. Mr. Davies stated, "There are other companies wanting to produce this book and I would be very happy to do business with you if you want to make it," or words to that effect. My brother made the deal with Mr. Davies to make it and it was at my brother's suggestion and not Mr. Davies.' I am rather surprised I said what I did, but I want to stand corrected, if I may.

Thus, J. L. Warner stood corrected on a matter that he once believed would never be made public. The Committee and he had been rather chummy in Los Angeles and the hearings there had ended on this note:

MR. STRIPLING: Doesn't it kind of provoke you to pay them $1,000 or $2,000 a week and see them on the picket lines and joining all of these organizations and taking your money and trying to tear down a system that provides the money?

MR. WARNER: That is absolutely correct. . . .

MR. STRIPLING: Your eyes have really been opened, Mr. Warner.

Entirely too open—in innocence—because soon afterward, when Warner had given his all. . . .

MR. THOMAS: Now, is there anything which you have given us that you would like for us to say to the press?

MR. WARNER: There is one thing that is very important, something I would not like to give to the press; let's put it that way.

MR. THOMAS: What is that?

MR. WARNER: That is the whole routine on *Mission to Moscow*. That is one thing I don't want to give to the press because that is like throwing the hammer and sickle up in front of you, and it all happened back in 1942.

All Thomas said was, "That's all. Witness excused." And now here was the testimony, hammer and sickle and all, spread on the public record.

Before J. L. Warner was allowed to leave the stand in Washington, there was a piece of business that had still not been finished to the Committee's satisfaction. It was the little business of the blacklist. It might be possible at this time to pin Warner down to something more definite.

Vail, the blacklist advocate, took over:

It would seem to me that this organization (Motion Picture Association) should concern itself with cleaning house in its own industry . . . through the elimination of writers and actors to whom definite Communistic leanings can be traced.

Don't you agree to that, Mr. Warner?

MR. WARNER: I agree to it personally, Mr. Congressman, but I cannot agree so far as the Association is concerned. I can't for the life of me figure where men could get together . . . to deprive a man of his livelihood because of his political beliefs. . . .

That, on Monday, October 20, 1947, before the hearings had a chance to get warmed up, seemed to settle the matter of blacklist in the motion picture industry. There were to be none, it seemed.

Eric Johnston, President of the Motion Picture Association, was not going to be intimidated by any congressional committee.

Not Johnston. . . .

The nineteen "unfriendly" men in the hearing room sent their congratulations to him.

"Tell the boys not to worry. There'll never be a blacklist. We're not going to go totalitarian to please this committee."

Fine words . . . American talk.

CHAPTER 4

"Is it your opinion that there were no political implications in it whatsoever?"

"I am convinced of that. I am under oath, and if I met my God I would still repeat the same thing."

METRO-GOLDWYN-MAYER is the biggest motion picture studio in the world. And Louis B. Mayer is the biggest man at M-G-M. He has the biggest office at the studio in Culver City; a private dining room, his personal chef and his own gymnasium and masseur. For a period of four years until 1945 his salary was the highest of any executive in the United States, in one year topping the million dollar mark.

His racing stables, until he sold them early in 1947, were the biggest in the West. His race-horses were the finest and the fastest and at one time during his career as a horse-breeder he made an offer to buy the late Man O' War, a gesture which did not sit well with race-lovers who regarded that animal as something of a national institution.

Oh, yes. Louis B. Mayer is big. But big as he is, before the House Un-American Activities Committee he was treated as pretty small potatoes.

Like J. L. Warner, his fellow-producer, Mayer came to the hearing with an intense desire to "clear up a misunderstanding." In Mayer's case, it was the circumstances surrounding his production, *Song of Russia,* in which Robert Taylor starred during the war. The Committee's attitude toward any motion picture regardless of when made, which said anything nice about the Soviet Union, was that it verged on high, cinematic treason.

But they would come to that, in time.

In the course of identifying himself, Mayer gave his birthplace as Russia. This bit of intelligence brought a score or more of random spectators forward in their seats. But he did not, as Warner did, give his age. He is in his late sixties, but elegantly dressed and barbered as he was, he looked not older than fifty. In response to Stripling's question as to his present occupation, please, he said, "I am head of the Metro-Goldwyn-Mayer Studios, Culver City, California."

H. A. Smith, one of the Committee's investigators, took over the questioning from there.

MR. SMITH: Could you give the Committee an idea of the gross income of Metro-Goldwyn-Mayer over 1 year, or over a number of years?

MR. MAYER: That I don't know, Mr. Smith.

For the information of Mr. Smith, Mr. Mayer, and our readers the net revenue of his company for 1944 was $145,121,000; for 1945, $154,230,000. The year 1946 was even better, and 1947 best of all.

The formal statement of L. B. Mayer began with a denunciation of Communism and an expression of how personally abhorrent it is to him. It proceeded to recount that he and his studio maintained a continuous vigilance lest any subversive idea ever creep into motion pictures which bear his lion trademark.

When he came to *Song of Russia,* he eased into it, after mentioning *Joe Smith, American* and *Mrs. Miniver.*

The statement was a masterpiece of special pleading, calculated to eliminate any suspicion that *Song of Russia* had even a smidgin of pro-Sovietism.

Robert Taylor had gotten the studio into this mess by the same kind of careless statements that J. L. Warner had made at the Los Angeles hearings of the Committee five months earlier. Taylor was fulsomely quoted by the press as claiming that irresistible "White House pressure" by "Roosevelt aides" had forced him into playing the leading role in this obnoxious motion picture, at a time when he, Taylor, was itching to fight Hitler.

How it actually came about that Taylor was "forced" into playing an American sympathetic to Russia was explained in Mayer's statement.

I thought Robert Taylor ideal for the male role, but he did not like the story. . . . At the time, Taylor mentioned his pending commission in the Navy, so I telephoned the Secretary of the Navy, Frank Knox, and told him of the situation, recalling the good that had been accomplished with *Mrs. Miniver* and other pictures released during the war period. The Secretary called back and said he thought Taylor could be given time to make the film before being called to the service.

That, and subsequent other denials that there was "White House pressure" or any other kind except the studio's eagerness to get the film finished, disposed of *Song of Russia* for the time being.

Mayer was a jump ahead of the Committee's already exposed intention to institute a blacklist, but somewhat behind Johnston and McNutt who had promised to fight such a move.

Mayer said:

It is my earnest hope that this Committee will perform a public service by recommending to the Congress legislation establishing a national policy regulating employment of Communists in private industry. It is my belief that they should be denied the sanctuary of the freedom they seek to destroy.

Later, in Congress, J. Parnell Thomas used almost the identical language in demanding that ten witnesses before him be cited for contempt.

MR. SMITH: Are there any Communists, to your knowledge, in Metro-Goldwyn-Mayer?

The answer to that question was nowhere in Mayer's written statement or in his memoranda. He was on his own, suddenly, and his response was a curious piece of circumlocution which attempted to say yes, no, and maybe in the same breath.

MR. MAYER: There is no proof about it, except they mark them as Communists, and when I look at the pictures they have written for us I can't find once where they have written something like that. Whether they think they can't get away with it in our place, or what,

[29]

I can't tell you. . . . I have as much contempt for them as anybody living in this world.

Which statement was of a piece with the logic of J. L. Warner: They can't prove these people are Communists. People say they are. Those Communists can't put a thing into pictures; they haven't yet. Here are the pictures as proof. They, the producers, hate them poisonously and kick them out forthwith.

Warner admitted that he accepted hearsay and trade-paper gossip as evidence of a writer's politics. Mayer quoted some mysterious oracle called "they" as his source.

They have mentioned two or three writers to me several times.
MR. SMITH: Who are these people they have named?

Mayer mentioned Dalton Trumbo and Lester Cole. Later, he recalled that "they" had also mentioned Donald Ogden Stewart.

Thereupon, Smith, who could get no reply at all as to the income of Metro-Goldwyn-Mayer, and was not concerned with the fabulous income of Louis B. Mayer himself, read into the record the amounts, to the last decimal point, those three writers earned at M-G-M.

MR. SMITH: Mr. Mayer, these individuals that have been mentioned as reported to you as Communists, do you think the studios should continue to employ those individuals?
MR. MAYER: I have asked counsel. They claim that unless you can prove they are Communists they can hold you for damages.

The Committee had enough theorizing and suggestions from Mayer. They yanked him back to the subject of *Song of Russia,* which, by this time, seemed quite obnoxious to the film magnate. At the persistent hinting by Smith that the picture "just did not depict Russia in one iota," Mayer bristled.

"We did not attempt to depict Russia," he declared, "we attempted to show a Russian girl entreating this American conductor to conduct a concert in her village . . . and as it inevitably happens this girl fell in love with the conductor and he with her. Then we showed the attack of the Germans on the Russians and the war disrupted this union."

[30]

Mayer appeared to be bored with the subject. But the Committee was just warming up. They asked Mayer who the writers were then when he couldn't recall, they furnished the names.

MR. SMITH: Did you read the first script, Mr. Mayer?
MR. MAYER: Yes, sir.
MR. SMITH: What was your opinion at that time?
MR. MAYER: They had farm collectivism in it and I threw it out. I will not preach any ideology except American and I don't even treat that. I let that take its own course and speak for itself.

Smith became interested in what Mayer's feelings were "as to the damage it might cause to the people of the United States, that is, misleading them as to conditions in Russia."
Mayer shrewdly asked, "What scenes are you referring to?"

MR. SMITH: Do you recall scenes in there at the night club where everybody was drinking.
MR. MAYER: They do in Moscow.
MR. SMITH: Do you feel that that represents Russia as it is today?
MR. MAYER: I didn't make it as it is today. I made it when they were our ally in 1943.

Having earlier secured the assurance that the Warner Brothers were working like beavers on an anti-Communist picture, the Committee asked Mr. Mayer what his studio was doing along the same line. He assured them that they were preparing to shoot *The Red Danube*. This, he explained, would be released under its original title, *Vespers in Vienna,* because the publishers of the novel insisted on it being that way.
What had Metro-Goldwyn-Mayer done about anti-Communist pictures in the past?
It had done nobly. Its productions *Ninotchka* and *Comrade X* were well ahead of the field.
"They kidded the life out of Communism in *Ninotchka*," said Mayer. "We kidded the pants off them in *Comrade X,* but they were not our allies then."
Mayer also explained that his studio made pictures with great American themes. One in particular:

We called that picture *American Romance,* in technicolor. It showed an immigrant coming by the Statue of Liberty. And through Ellis Island, he walks out to Minnesota to the iron mines, where he has some relations—walking across the country getting a ride here and there. He becomes a Henry Ford under our system which makes that possible. He became a great industrialist.

Mr. Stripling took over. There was no subtlety about his technique which jolted Mayer back to *Song of Russia.* He wanted Mayer's assurance that there was no political implications whatever, and it was here that Mr. Mayer said, "I am convinced of that. I am under oath, and if I met my God, I would still repeat the same thing."

And it was at this point too that Mr. Mayer was asked to step down—to make way for somebody who *really* knew what political implications were—Miss Ayn Rand.

Miss Rand identified herself first, as an emigré from Russia who came here in 1926 and has not returned to her native Muscovy since. She held different views regarding *Song of Russia* from those of Mr. Mayer. She testified that she had viewed the picture recently, courtesy of the Thomas Committee, and found it loaded with Communist propaganda.

It starts with Robert Taylor playing the American national anthem and the national anthem dissolves into a Russian mob with the sickle and the hammer on a red flag very prominently above their heads . . . that was a terrible touch of propaganda . . . it suggests literally and technically that it is quite alright for the American national anthem to dissolve into the Soviet.
. . . Now we go to the pleasant love story. . . .

She used that last phrase mockingly, not tenderly as Louis B. Mayer used it when he described that little masterpiece.

From there on, Miss Rand took over the hearing with a gloveless hand of iron, and no holds barred.

Miss Rand spoke an estimated three thousand words before any members of the Committee could insert a word in edgewise or otherwise. In her view, Louis B. Mayer was not much better than an agent of a foreign government inasmuch as the film he produced showed the Russians smiling, which Miss Rand said, "is one of the stock propaganda tricks of the Communists—to show these people smiling." The presence of neat, clean cottages in the picture appalled her.

Rep. Wood asked her, "Do you think, then, that it was to our advantage or to our disadvantage to keep Russia in this war at the time this picture was made?"

MISS RAND: That has absolutely nothing to do with what we are discussing.

MR. WOOD: Well—

MISS RAND: But if you want me to answer, I can answer, but it will take me a long time to say what I think as to whether we should or should not have had Russia on our side in the war.

Mr. Wood remarked that there is a pretty strong probability that we wouldn't have won at all if Russia had not been our ally.

MISS RAND: I don't know, because on the other hand, I think we could have used the lend-lease supplies that we sent there to much better advantage ourselves.

What followed was a sharp little debate on military and foreign policy between the witness and Mr. Wood. The committeeman managed to interject five complete sentences and three "wells" as opposed to about four hundred words from Miss Rand in which she painted a dismal picture of the Soviet Union.

MR. McDOWELL: You came here in 1926, I believe you said. Did you escape from Russia?

MISS RAND: No.

MR. McDOWELL: Did you have a passport?

MISS RAND: No. Strangely enough they gave me a passport to come out here as a visitor . . . it was at a time when they relaxed their orders a little bit. . . . I was permitted to come here for a year. I never went back.

As Miss Rand returned to her seat after leaving the witness stand, she passed Mr. Mayer, who she had given such a raking over. They did not speak.

CHAPTER 5

*"Mr. Wood, to use the slang expression, you
really lay it on the line. . . . In other words
you've got guts."*

*"Thank you very much. You will find the
men in our organization have the same, sir."*

THE gutty organization referred to in this exchange of compliments is the Motion Picture Alliance for the Preservation of
Americal Ideals which was formed in Hollywood early in 1944.
In the Congressional Record of March 7, that year, former
Senator Robert Rice Reynolds inserted a communication received by him which purported to give in a nutshell the principles of this Alliance. . . . "Because of the flagrant manner
in which the motion picture industrialists of Hollywood have
been coddling Communists and co-operating with the so-called
intellectual superiors they have helped to import from Europe
and Asia, there has been organized in Hollywood, the Motion
Picture Alliance."

Samuel Grosvenor Wood, the noted motion picture director,
was one of the founding members of the Alliance and its first
president. A dozen "friendly" witnesses who followed him to
the stand in Washington were members and officers of that
organization—with guts.

In the four years of its existence, the MPA-for-the-PAI allied
itself concurrently with the producing heads of the film studios
and the House Un-American Activities Committee. With only
minor changes in its text, the Alliance statement of principles
was used in 1944 by the Hollywood for Dewey Committee and
in 1948 by the Hollywood Republican Committee.

On the cultural and ideological role of the Alliance, Carey
McWilliams, the noted sociologist and author of *Southern California Country,* recently said, "The Alliance would have the

public believe that films devoid of ideas are also films devoid of propaganda. What they have been aiming at, from the outset, is a censorship of films controlled by those with whom they are in alliance—The Un-American Activities Committee."

The fact of collaboration between the Thomas Committee and the Alliance could no longer be denied the minute Miss Rand assumed the witness stand in Washington.

Again referring to the political holy-rolling activities of the Alliance, McWilliams described it as, "An absurd and revolting spectacle, indeed; but a dangerous one also. For the Alliance itself is shot through with self-hatred, the blind, mole-like fear of change, the deep-seated social envy and sense of personal inadequacy, the cheap cynicism and the psuedo-hardboiled know-nothingism of those who cannot imagine the existence of values really worth defending and who traduce, by their every act and statement, the basic American ideals."

Samuel Grosvenor Wood and Robert E. Stripling worked with a precision which could have been bettered only by a dress rehearsal. For a long stretch the questions and answers had a "Mr. Bones and Interlocutor" quality.

Mr. STRIPLING: What group in the industry must be watched more carefully than the rest?

Mr. WOOD: The writers.

Mr. STRIPLING: Would you care to name any that you know yourself to be Communists?

Mr. Wood did—Trumbo, Stewart, Lawson, on the grounds that when the *Hollywood Reporter* asked them, "Are you Communist?" they refused to answer.

Mr. STRIPLING: These groups or cliques that you have referred to . . . are they a source of financial assistance to the Communist Party?

Right on cue, Mr. Wood answered, "Very substantial. For example, at a rally which Katharine Hepburn attended, they raised $87,000—and you know that didn't go to the Boy Scouts."

Katharine Hepburn not only attended, Wood may well recall, but literally seared the ears off the Motion Picture Alliance for the Preservation of American Ideals. And the occasion was a testimonial meeting for Henry A. Wallace just returned from a European tour.

Wood also expertized on the foreign market, with particular emphasis on Russia's disinclination to import *Grapes of Wrath* for exhibition, because the Soviet citizens might be jealous of their Okie betters, who

. . . poor as they were, they did have a piece of ground, and they did have an automobile, and they are at liberty to get the automobile and travel across the country.

A final word from Mr. Wood on how the governmental processes can be attacked in motion pictures by the wrong kind of writers:

. . . I think it is particularly bad if that is constantly shown, every night you go to the pictures you see a dishonest banker, or senator, you begin to think that the whole system is wrong.

Bored, perhaps, with answering yes or no to specific questions as to whether in their opinion certain people were Communists, occasional friendly witnesses used quaint locutions. When asked, "Is there any question in your mind as to whether Lawson is a Communist?" he replied, "If there is, then I haven't any mind."

Morrie Ryskind, who admitted that he had once, in his salad days as a confused liberal, donated money to the defense of the Scottsboro victims and to the cause of freeing Tom Mooney, was asked by Stripling about the politics of another writer. Ryskind's answer was, "If he isn't a Communist, I don't think Mahatma Gandhi is an Indian."

Later, Fred Niblo, Jr., another stalwart of the Motion Picture Alliance, chose to respond in the same quaint way when asked about another writer. He said, "I can't prove that he is a Communist any more than Custer could prove that the people who were massacring him were Indians."

Ryskind, after flailing about him for twenty minutes, denounced other writers, took occasion to solemnly warn:

[36]

They use the techniques of character assassination, and if they ever get control of the screen or of the country, it won't be just characters they will assassinate.

He had many additional suggestions to give the producers from this tribune, but J. Parnell Thomas thought Ryskind had done well enough. Would he kindly step down.

By mid-morning of the second day of testimony, the newspapermen covering the event began to have that lean, copy-hungry look which meant that their editors were clamoring for a "new lead" or a fresh story. Adolphe Menjou had been on the stand and was gone. He was photogenic in appearance and florid in his testimony. But his disclosures described in a later chapter had not held up for more than one edition.

Whereupon, the Thomas Committee broke out John Charles Moffit, a motion picture critic who said that he "accepts employment" as a scenario writer. Mr. Moffit, the Junior G-Man of the "friendly" witnesses promptly furnished the thirsting press with two bouncy headlines. First, his considered findings that the New York stage was breeding grounds of Communistic propaganda and that a theater-piece that did not have a subversive theme was doomed. The second bombshell was something right out of a comic book.

Quoting from a fat dossier which Moffit carried to the stand, he solemnly charged that a young test pilot named Chalmers (Slick) Goodlin was tricked by a Communist *provocateur,* in the guise of a literary agent, into disclosing the secret of the latest supersonic war plane.

"Early in the Spring," Moffit related, "Goodlin came to Hollywood on a visit. . . ."

And here a literary scout for a talent agency (or so he called himself) and "a number of people of strong left-wing tendencies got to the boy."

Moffit continued:

They told him that one engaged in his activity should most certainly have a wonderful story to sell to the magazines. I understand that he replied that anything he wrote would have to be passed through military intelligence. The reply was, "Oh, of course that will be done, but

[37]

let us see a sample of what you can write and we will see whether it is admissible."

The boy was foolish enough to do this, and his story, his draft of a magazine article containing, as I understand it, much confidential information on the supersonic plane came into the hands of Mr. Weber, the literary agent who was sent to Hollywood by Communist Headquarters in New York.

Before Mr. Moffit tottered off the stand the Hearst, McCormick, and the Patterson presses were reeling with the sensation.

But not many hours later, some of the same newspapers published an interview with the same test pilot in which he said, "I don't know where this man Moffit got his information but he certainly got it all wrong. It's the sheerest kind of nonsense."

From the roster of the Motion Picture Alliance for the Preservation of American Ideals, the Committee fetched up its most literate member, James K. McGuinness, one of that organization's founders and still its principal theoretician. In his activity at Metro-Goldwyn-Mayer, he said that he "exercises a general editorial supervision over a proportion of the scripts prepared for production in that studio," which shows how fine executive responsibility is shaved in Culver City.

Early in his testimony, Mr. McGuinness was asked by the Investigator-of-the-day, Mr. Smith, if he thought that anti-Communist pictures should be made. He replied that he did. Some 8,000 words later, Mr. McGuinness remarked that the screen is an "awkward medium for political debate." He also said that he would be reluctant to see "legislation directed at anyone for his political beliefs." But a few adroit questions later eked from him a recommendation for the passage of just such legislation.

With an admirable clarity he stated that, in his opinion, the outlawing of a political belief serves no purpose. "I don't think a law overcomes an idea," he said.

This, naturally, did not sit well with the Committee which has several laws designed to overcome a like number of ideas. So, before Mr. McGuinness descended from the stand he joined hands with them and took that issue out of the realm of controversy.

"You have been a splendid witness," J. Parnell Thomas said to him in parting.

An equally splendid witness in the Committee's terms was Richard Macauley, a screen writer. For weeks before the subpoenas descended upon Hollywood, Macauley had been bursting with things to tell the Un-American Committee. He had been overlooked in the preliminary examination of friendly witnesses. So, when his subpoena was finally handed to him, Macauley was the happiest man on the Metro-Goldwyn lot.

He had come to smear the Screen Writers' Guild in which he was even then one of the three candidates for president. He dipped the brush often and with enthusiasm. He promptly declared that this Guild, whose affairs and policies are directed by an executive board which is elected by the secret ballot of the membership, to be dominated by a controlling faction; a well-organized clique who he identified as "the Communists and the boys who play along with them."

MR. SMITH: Are you able to identify some of these individuals, in your opinion?

MR. MACAULEY: Oh, yes.

MR. SMITH: Will you do so?

MR. MACAULEY: A lot of these people—a few of them may not be Communists. I might possibly be doing an injustice to some of them.

MR. SMITH: We would prefer that you name only those in the Guild whom you feel are Communists.

MR. MACAULEY: I am morally certain of all of them. I merely say if they habitually consort with bank robbers and the bank on the next street is knocked off they can't holler if someone blows the whistle.

Whereupon Macauley blew it, in rough alphabetic order, twenty-eight times.

CHAPTER 6

*"We haven't received a rouble from Russia
on either picture. . . . I think I have a character
in there they do not like." "Bing Crosby?" "No;
God."*

NOWHERE in the entire hearings did the proceedings appear
less impromptu, less spontaneous, more carefully staged than in
the testimony of Leo McCarey, producer and director of *Going
My Way* and *The Bells of St. Mary's*. As a result of the fantastic
box-office returns these two film dramas brought in, McCarey,
in recent income tax disclosures became the highest salaried
man in America, nosing Louis B. Mayer out for that distinc-
tion.

In the Caucus Room of the Old House Office Building, the
exchange of patter between him and Stripling sounded as if it
had been written and rehearsed. There were the proper "feeder
lines" for the straight man and the "zingers" for the comedian.

MR. STRIPLING: Were *Going My Way* and *Bells of St. Mary's* two
of the most popular pictures which you have produced in recent years,
according to the box-office?

MR. McCAREY: According to the box-office they were both very successful.

MR. STRIPLING: They did very well?

MR. McCAREY: Yes, sir.

MR. STRIPLING: How did they do in Russia?

MR. McCAREY: We haven't received one rouble from Russia on
either picture.

MR. STRIPLING: What is the trouble?

MR. McCAREY: Well, I think I have a character in there they do
not like.

MR. STRIPLING: Bing Crosby?

MR. McCAREY: No; God.

With this somewhat irreverent "yock," the Committee and Leo McCarey furnished the radio and the newspapers with the homely little feature of the day.

The rest of Mr. McCarey's testimony was tepid, routine, perfunctory—a rather weary repetition of the questions and answers which had been heard in these chambers so many, many times.

The writers were the target as usual.

Yes, Mr. McCarey had noticed the activities of Communists in a particular group—the writers' group. Yes, that was the principal medium for the injection of un-American or the suppression of pro-American ideas—though what these ideas might be, Mr. McCarey didn't say.

For a mild novelty he included the casting directors—those responsible for choosing an actor to fit a particular part.

MR. McCAREY: The dialogue in the script could be ostensibly quite innocuous but they can cast a character so repulsive when you take one look at him you don't like the man who is portrayed as a capitalist, a banker, or whatever part he is portraying.

In the naive belief that a banker was a hallowed American institution, Stripling asked McCarey if he didn't think there was danger in film portrayals of such "institutions in a disparaging light." In other words . . .

. . . if pictures are made which always have the banker as the heavy . . . and that picture is shown in foreign countries, Europe and so on, what do you think the ultimate effect would be?

MR. McCAREY: Well, naturally, it would give a very unfavorable opinion of people who are successful in the United States.

MR. STRIPLING: Do you think that is a dangerous practice for the motion pictures to pursue?

McCarey thought it would be a very dangerous practice.

Both McCarey and Stripling overlooked the fact that the banker in Mr. McCarey's production *Going My Way* was an arch villain who threatened to foreclose the mortgage, not merely on the pitiful hovel of a poor widow, but on a property where stood a Catholic church.

[41]

Had Mr. McCarey personal encounters with Communist writers seeking to place propaganda in his pictures? Indeed he had.

Would Mr. McCarey detail such an instance?

Well, Mr. McCarey wasn't so good with the details. About all he could come up with was the eternally belabored pronoun "they."

"They" would throw cold water on Mr. McCarey's ideas if those ideas didn't agree with "their" policy.

"They" were always giving Mr. McCarey books to read, causing Mr. McCarey to maintain a painful alertness in order to detect the latest propaganda in these books.

"Is it very subtle, in other words?" Mr. Stripling tenderly inquired.

"At times very subtle," Mr. McCarey sighed. It appeared that some of "them" were very clever.

That was all from Mr. Stripling. The wearied Committeemen had no questions but J. Parnell Thomas, the Chairman, had a few.

Did Mr. McCarey think the industry should produce anti-Communist films?

Mr. McCarey was vague. Far from explicit. He bumbled. He felt that the screen was a great art. That Donald Duck was a great hero. That films should be entertainment. That they should be held to a level of what the medium stands for. That the *Three Little Pigs* was very successful. That pictures should not take any sides at all.

"In other words you believe we would be doing the same thing—" the Chairman tried to break in.

But Mr. McCarey was still engaged in his philosophic reverie. "We would," he said, "bring on more bitterness, I think."

Not to be denied, the Chairman pressed his point. "We would be doing the same thing Soviet Russia is doing?" J. Parnell Thomas insisted.

Without pausing to inquire whether Mr. Thomas had reference to Russian films or to the councils of the United Nations, McCarey obligingly replied, "That is right."

The Chairman addressed McCarey as "one of the leaders or

spokesmen of your profession, spokesman for a great many people." Although who these hypothetical masses of people might be seemed to be the last thing on the Congressman's mind.

As such a spokesman, Thomas wished to know, did McCarey favor the outlawing by Congress of the Communist Party of the United States.

McCarey did. His reply, while cheerfully co-operative, gave a generally confusing effect. He thought that within the confines of the United States we could have all the parties we want— he made them sound rather like square dances or Maypole rings—we could have healthy debate on any subject for the betterment of all peoples, but he didn't think we should align ourselves with any "foreign" party.

With some prompting from the Chairman, Mr. McCarey agreeably stated that he thought American Communists were agents of a foreign government. Then he grew wistful.

"It seems," he said pensively, "like in a way some people accuse us of being afraid of mentioning names."

He thought it would be nice if we had a law somewhere along the line under Treason, subdivision D, or "something like that." Then he would be very happy to mention names.

"So that if there was a law on the books making the Communist Party illegal," said the Congressman sternly, "you would not hesitate to name persons whom you know and believe to be Communists?"

"That is right," Mr. McCarey agreed again and stepped down.

It was to be noted that the House Committee on Un-American Affairs acted with Bourbon punctilio toward the two "friendly" ladies whom it had subpoenaed—Miss Ayn Rand and Mrs. Lela Rogers. Neither was asked to tell her age.

Mrs. Rogers informed the world that she was born in Council Bluffs, Iowa, but she didn't say when.

She softly admitted that she was the mother of Ginger Rogers, film actress, but she didn't repeat her now famous and outraged declaration to the Committee at the earlier hearing; that the line her daughter had been asked to say in a scene for a motion picture; "Share and share alike—that's democracy!" was subversive, dangerous and clearly Communist propaganda.

In fact, she never succeeded in reaching the height of that earlier pronouncement, although she tried.

In her role of guardian and censor over what was suitable for the public mind, she told how courageously she fought to prevent RKO Studios, a large corporation from producing a vehicle of "open Communist propaganda" called *None But the Lonely Heart,* starring Cary Grant.

This gallant struggle went down to defeat, leaving Mrs. Rogers to fight a desperate rear-guard action against the employment of Clifford Odets to write the screenplay for the picture.

My objection to Mr. Odets as a writer was that for years I had heard that Mr. Odets was a Communist.

MR. STRIPLING: What do you base that upon?

MRS. ROGERS: I have here a column of Mr. O. O. McIntyre datelined Jan. 8, 1936, in which Mr. McIntyre says Mr. Clifford Odets, play writer, is a member of the Communist Party. I never saw that denied.

In support of her contention that *None But the Lonely Heart* was Communistic, Mrs. Rogers offered a quote from a critique of the picture in the *Hollywood Reporter:* ". . . story, pitched in a low key, is moody and somber throughout in the Russian manner."

Mr. McDowell, the Committee member from Pennsylvania, asked Mrs. Rogers what she would "describe in this film as being Communist propaganda."

MRS. ROGERS: I will tell you of one line. The mother in the story runs a second-hand store. The son says to her, "You are not going to" —in essence, I am not quoting this exactly, because I can't remember it exactly—"You are not going to get me to work here and squeeze pennies out of little people who are poorer than we are."

Mrs. Rogers added, "We don't necessarily squeeze pennies from people poorer than we are. Many people are poorer and many people are richer."

[44]

Mr. Vail, questioned doubtfully the effectiveness of the "Hollywood Communists," estimated by some witnesses as one per cent.

Mrs. Rogers looked up, and as though bestowing an emerald on him, said, "You are thinking like an American, sir."

After receiving the compliments of the Committee for "lending her great talents" as "one of the outstanding experts on Communism in the United States, and particularly in the amusement industry," plus its tenderly solicitous apologies for having brought her all the way from Hollywood to perform her heroic task of enlightening the American press and people, Mrs. Rogers flounced gracefully from the stand.

Full of years and honors, the eminent Rupert Hughes took the stand and fought as doughtily against "the left" as ever he did in the columns of the Hearst newspapers or at revival meetings of the Hollywood Authors Club. It was overlooked generally by the press that he was the uncle of Howard Hughes, the young millionaire planebuilder who wreaked confusion in the ranks of an earlier congressional committee.

Uncle Rupert's (he is called that by a tight little coterie of litterateurs in Hollywood) most recent public utterance had to do with the Four Freedoms. He was against them on the grounds that "they would rob the American people of the stimulus of fear and poverty."

As a witness before the Thomas Committee he was heart and soul with them, but Mr. Stripling had considerable difficulty in keeping him to the point.

For example, when Mr. Stripling was attempting to find out from Mr. Hughes what members, if any, of the Screen Writers Guild Mr. Hughes discerned to be closely associated with the Communists, Mr. Hughes discussed wolves.

Yes. You can't help smelling them in a way. Their ideas are all one way. I have had furious debates with Emmet Lavery in forums and privately. . . . Lavery is a good Catholic, he says, but I say a man whose views are Communist, whose friends are Communists and whose work is Communistic, is a Communist. I would say if a wolf wears sheep's clothing, that man is a wolf.

[45]

At another point in the course of his voluble, if rambling response to the same question, he said, "That is the way I tell a Communist. A man who never says a word against the bloodiest butcher in history, Stalin, and who says violent words against the most modest American. That is my test."

Mr. Stripling attempted to learn from Mr. Hughes whether the latter thought that the Committee was trying to impose thought control. That, Mr. Hughes replied, nearly made him die laughing. But many words later Mr. Hughes was still replying while Mr. Stripling visibly wilted. With his eyes closed, Mr. Hughes was intoning:

. . . I think any Communist is an enemy spy or agent. . . . They are worse than Benedict Arnold. They are fighting every effort anyone has made. They tried to force me out of the Authors League as well as others. I know anti-Communist writers in Hollywood who have been forced practically to starvation by the refusal of the Communist writers to work for them.

MR. STRIPLING: Mr. Hughes, who are the people in Hollywood that you feel could do the most to thwart the activities of the Communists?

Now Mr. Hughes, who is seventy-five, unfortunately does not hear very well and apparently all he grasped from this question was the word "Communists."

MR. HUGHES: I think their names have been mentioned here numerous times. I would subscribe to all of them. I have a poor memory. You read them to me and I can give you my opinion of them.

MR. STRIPLING: I am afraid you misunderstood my question. I will rephrase it. Who would the responsibility rest with for cleaning the Communists out of the motion picture industry?

MR. HUGHES: Well, I think the producers in general should do it because they are the people who hire and fire. I think they have been unjustifiably lax. They have paid from two thousand to five thousand dollars a week to men whom they know to be brilliant. Many Communists are very, very brilliant.

It was the last compliment he paid them for the balance of his all-too-brief hour on the stand.

CHAPTER 7

"I believe that under certain circumstances a Communistic director, a Communistic writer, or a Communistic actor, even if he were under orders from the head of the studio not to inject Communism or un-Americanism or subversion into pictures, could easily subvert that order, under the proper circumstances, by a look, by an inflection, by a change in the voice, I think it could be easily done. I have never seen it done, but I think it could be done."

IN his thirty-four years as a motion picture actor, Adolphe Jean Menjou (born in Pittsburgh fifty-seven years ago) has tied down pretty securely the title of the screen's best-dressed mummer.

In his testimony before the House Un-American Activities Committee he revealed that he has now set his sights on higher accolades, and aims to be known as the best-read member of his profession. Indeed, he allowed the Committee to pry from him the information that he had read over 450 books on one subject—Russia, or as he prefers to call it, "an oriental tyranny, a Kremlin-dominated conspiracy."

In the years Mr. Menjou has given to the cinema he has appeared in more than a hundred pictures, from *The Sheik* through *Are Parents People?* right down to *Bachelor's Daughters*. During this time he has accumulated a considerable amount of money, and although part of it has gone into his tweeds and his tomes, the major portion of it—much of which was gathered in during the low income tax years—rests comfortably in the vaults of a highly solvent Hollywood bank.

Despite his personal wealth and obvious security—or possibly because of it—Mr. Menjou's heart bleeds for "the poor Russian peasants" starving, as he puts it in his testimony, "en masse" and "the masses of Russian officers who have come to the American headquarters and asked how they can get into America . . . the Russian general who is now in Buenos Aires . . . the young senior lieutenant who tried to commit suicide rather than to return to his country."

Too grief-stricken to verify his statements or to name the unfortunate militarists, Mr. Menjou nevertheless plainly stamped himself as a man with a heart as big as all Beverly Hills.

Testifying before the Committee in a blue double-breasted pin-striped suit, Mr. Menjou got right down to work in his role as a "student of Communism."

At the outset he declared that he had made "a particular study of Marxism, Fabian Socialism, Communism, Stalinism, and its probable effects on the American people, if they ever gain power here." Questioned by Mr. Stripling as to his first-hand observance of Communist propaganda in motion pictures, Mr. Menjou was constrained to say that "I have seen no Communistic propaganda in pictures—if you mean 'vote for Stalin,' or that type of Communistic propaganda."

As a matter of fact, Mr. Menjou said he didn't "like that term 'Communist propaganda,' because I have seen no such thing as Communist propaganda, such as waving the hammer and sickle in motion pictures. I have seen things that I thought were against what I considered good Americanism, in my feeling. I have seen pictures I thought shouldn't have been made— shouldn't have been made, let me put it that way."

MR. STRIPLING: Mr. Menjou, do you have any particular pictures in mind—

MR. MENJOU: Well—

MR. STRIPLING: When you make that statement?

MR. MENJOU: Well, I wonder if I could preface it by a short statement?

MR. STRIPLING: Yes, if you please.

MR. MENJOU: I am not here to smear. I am here to defend the industry, that I have spent the greater part of my life in. I am here to defend the producers and the motion-picture industry.

[48]

Mr. Thomas repeated in tones of great sincerity and sonorousness that smearing the screen was farthest from his thoughts.

When Mr. Menjou got around to naming the pictures he thought shouldn't have been made, he could do no better than two old whipping boys of the Committee, *Mission to Moscow* and *North Star*. Nor did he "know any members of the Screen Actors Guild who are members of the Communist Party," but he knew some "who act an awful lot like Communists."

Pressed for examples, Mr. Menjou dug up, not an actor, but a director, Mr. John Cromwell. Mr. Cromwell, according to Mr. Menjou,

... in his own house, said to me that capitalism in America was through and I would see the day when it was ended in America. A very strange statement from a man who earns upward of $250,000 a year, who owns a great deal of Los Angeles and Hollywood real estate. It is rather difficult to reconcile that. He is profiting by the capitalistic system, and yet he is against it. He told me so with his own lips.

Prodded by Mr. Stripling for further "observations regarding Communist activity in Hollywood in the past 10 years," Mr. Menjou really opened the vast library of his mind. He yielded to no man in his knowledge of Communism acquired mainly by reading.

MR. MENJOU: I have a list of books here—I published a list of over 35 books—and if you will bear with me and if I have the time I would like to read a list of books which I would advise every man, woman, and child in America to read. They will then get a picture of this oriental tyranny, this Communist-dominated conspiracy to take the world over by force. It will take the words out of Mr. Lenin's mouth, out of Mr. Stalin's mouth. Mr. Molotov is a member of the Politburo. Mr. Vishinsky I consider simply a puppet.

Here are some titles of Mr. Menjou's reading list "for every man, woman and child in America." The blurbs are his own.

Das Kapital, by Karl Marx and the Max Eastman condensation;

A magnificent book called *The Red Prussian;*

[49]

Towards Soviet America, by William Z. Foster. You will have trouble getting the book. You will have to advertise for it.

Dark Side of the Moon. I defy anyone to read that without being frightened to death.

Over at Uncle Joe's, a magnificent book by Atkinson;

and one of the best books of all, *Pattern for World Revolution,* written anonymously.

"This," he said, "is only a very, very small list of books, but I guarantee you that any one that reads them will fear for the safety of America."

There was more, a lot more. And the Committee was not unappreciative. As Mr. McDowell, one of its members, put it, "Mr. Menjou, I believe I told you last May, on the West Coast, that of all the thousands of people I have discussed Communism with, you have the most profound knowledge of the background of Communism I have ever met."

Mr. Menjou rose to the compliment with a new burst of un-documented oratory. "The Russian people are completely enslaved," he declaimed. "Mr. Vishinsky is enslaved. Mr. Molotov is enslaved. They are all frightened to death. Mr. Stalin would just as soon kill them as look at them. He killed all his close friends. There is excellent evidence that he poisoned Lenin, Gorky, and that he also executed the pharmacist, the head of the NKVD at the time, who was the witness. He acted very much like Mr. Capone. He committed the murders and then killed the witnesses."

For this startling bit of news, Mr. Menjou was once more saluted by Mr. McDowell, who said, "Mr. Chairman, in addition to being a great American, here is one of the greatest American patriots I have ever met."

Warmed by this simple tribute, Mr. Menjou found it in his heart to express sympathy for fellow-actors who do not share his viewpoint. "I believe they are innocent dupes," he offered generously. "That is my impression of them, innocent dupes."

But his sympathy stopped short of anyone "attending any meetings at which Mr. Paul Robeson appeared and applauding or listening to his Communist songs in America." Mr. Menjou said he "would be ashamed to be seen in an audience doing a thing of that kind."

Once more Mr. Menjou was steered back to Communism in Hollywood, this time by the Committee's Mr. Nixon.

MR. NIXON: What if a producer is informed that a writer he has in his employ is a member of the Communist Party, what should his action be?

MR. MENJOU: He could be very carefully watched; this producer could watch every script and every scene of every script. We have many Communist writers who are splendid writers. They do not have to write communistically at all, but they have to be watched.

Beyond eternal vigilance, Mr. Menjou had no suggestions for coping with Communist propaganda in pictures, which he had previously denied existed.

In the stretch now, Mr. Menjou was yet not too winded to denounce "certain individuals" who had purportedly declared that the hearings of the Committee threatened censorship of the screen.

It is perfectly infantile to say this committee is trying to control the industry. How could they possibly control the industry? They wouldn't know anything about it. You wouldn't know how to make a picture or anything else. I don't see how that could be said by any man with the intelligence of a louse.

Mr. Menjou declared himself unafraid of Communism, and at the same time stated his plans in case it ever overtook America. "I would move to the state of Texas if it ever came here," he said, "because I think the Texans would kill them on sight."

Even Texas was not immune, according to the Committee's Mr. McDowell, who said, "I would like to tell Mr. Menjou something to add to his already great knowledge of Communism. Recently I have been examining the borders of the United States. I would like to tell you, Mr. Menjou, that within weeks, not months but weeks, bus loads of Communists have crossed the American border."

Mr. Menjou readily agreed, and added something to Mr. McDowell's already great knowledge of borders. "There was a great, profitable industry in smuggling Chinese over the border," Mr. Menjou stated. "One of my good friends made a great deal of money doing it."

Getting away from his good friend and back to himself for the finish, Mr. Menjou declared:

I believe America should arm to the teeth. I believe in universal military training. I attended Culver Military Academy during the last war and enlisted as a private. Due to my military training I was soon made an officer and it taught me a great many things. I believe if I was told to swim the Mississippi River I would learn how to swim. Every young man should have military training. There is no better thing for a young man than military training for his discipline, for his manhood, for his courage, and for love of his country. I know it was good for me. It never did me any harm.

Unharmed, Mr. Menjou left the stand.

The story of Robert Taylor's rise in Hollywood is so typical of the movie industry's way with a boy or girl born beautiful and pliant that it long ago ceased to interest the film news writers.

Born Spangler Arlington Brugh in Filley, Nebraska, in 1911, he found his way in his late teens to Pomona College. Seen there in an amateur show by Metro-Goldwyn-Mayer talent scouts, he was tested, contracted, coached, beautified and publicized, rushed into leading-man roles which brought him in two years the fattest parts on the biggest movie lot in town, a place among the Big Ten box-office draws, and a spotlighted marriage to Barbara Stanwyck.

No one would have noticed had Spangler Arlington Brugh, of Filley, Nebraska, spoken out against gasoline rationing, income taxes and Roosevelt. But Robert Taylor's opinions made news.

His appearance before the House Un-American Activities

Committee involved interest above and beyond the gasps of
the graying Congressional secretaries who followed him around
during his stay in Washington.

Taylor's statement before the Committee's preview hearing in
Hollywood in the spring that he had been "forced" by a Roosevelt emissary to play the American conductor who looked with
friendly eyes on collective farmers in *Song of Russia,* had brought
angry denials from Lowell Mellett, wartime chief of the Bureau
of Motion Pictures, Office of War Information, whom Taylor
had indicated as the man with the thumb screws.

Newsmen, who had heard much talk but seen little action,
were hoping that—unless Taylor set their record straight—
Mellett might sue.

But Taylor set the record straight.

If he ever gave the impression in anything that he had said
previously that he was forced into making *Song of Russia,* he
wished to say:

. . . in my own defense, lest I look a little silly by saying I was ever
forced to do the picture, I was not forced because nobody can force
you to make any picture.

I objected to it, but in deference to the situation as it then existed
I did the picture.

He "did not believe" that it was made at the suggestion of a
Government representative.

"No, sir. I think the script was written and prepared long
before any representative of the Government became involved in
it in any way."

Had he been present at a meeting at which "a representative
of the Government was present and this picture was discussed?"

MR. TAYLOR: Yes sir; in Mr. L. B. Mayer's office. One day I was
called to meet Mr. Mellett whom I met in the company of Mr. Mayer,
and, as I recall, the *Song of Russia* was discussed briefly. I don't think
we were together more than 5 minutes.

So the story of New Deal "dictatorship" to Hollywood, like
so many of the one-edition sensations which boiled up in the
Committee room, was dead.

But Mr. Taylor who said he had been "looking for Communism for a long time," had a few opinions to add to the record on the subject of Red infiltration of the movie industry.

"In the past four or five years, specifically," he said, "I have seen more indications which seemed to me to be signs of Communistic activity in Hollywood and the motion picture industry."

MR. STRIPLING: In any particular field?

MR. TAYLOR: No, sir. I suppose the most readily determined field in which it could be cited would be in the preparation of scripts—specifically, in the writing of those scripts. I have seen things from time to time which appeared to me to be slightly on the pink side, shall we say; at least, that was my personal opinion.

He named one writer, Lester Cole, "who is reputedly a Communist. I would not know personally."

He named two actors who "if they are not Communists they are working awfully hard to be Communists."

But, like Mr. Menjou, he didn't *know*.

Pressed for personal knowledge of scripts which "contained any lines of material which you considered might be un-American or Communistic—any lines which you objected to"—he thought hard, and came up with an affirmative reply.

MR. TAYLOR: Oh, yes, sir. I think from time to time you are bound to run into lines and situations and scenes which I would consider objectionable. One script was submitted to me quite some time ago, but not officially from the studio, which I objected to on the basis that it seemed to foster ideologies which I did not personally agree with.

However, nothing more came out of it. The script has not been made and I have heard nothing about it, as a matter of fact.

But he did believe that Communistic activity in Hollywood had "definitely increased" following Pearl Harbor. "The ground work for their work in this country was obviously more fertile."

As for himself, however, Mr. Taylor put it very forthrightly. He had never joined any Communist-front organization.

"No, sir; believe me."

He had not, to his knowledge, ever "played in any picture with people whom you had any doubts about their loyalty to the Government."

He had never "worked with anyone knowingly who is a Communist. Moreover, I shall never work with anyone who is a Communist."

MR. STRIPLING: You would refuse to act in a picture in which a person whom you considered to be a Communist was also cast; is that correct?

MR. TAYLOR: I most assuredly would and I would not even have to know that he was a Communist. This may sound biased; however, if I were even suspicious of a person being a Communist with whom I was scheduled to work, I am afraid it would have to be him or me, because life is a little too short to be around people who annoy me as much as these fellow travelers and Communists do.

Authors of *The High Wall,* the motion picture upon which Mr. Taylor had just finished work, as it turned out, were Sidney Boehm—and Lester Cole!

There is a story going the rounds among Hollywood literati which characterizes the strong, silent, handsome and shy woman-killer whom Gary Cooper has made a film stereotype.

It is told about Gary himself, who was sent galley proofs, hot off the presses, of a new novel which his studio hoped to buy for a Cooper starring vehicle.

Competition for the property was fevered, and after a few days—with no report from Cooper—a studio executive called to prod him for his opinion.

"Great story for you, isn't it?" The questioner was eager.

"Yup."

"Great finish, when you ride off into the sunset with the girl."

"Didn't get that far yet."

"Oh." There was a pause. Then the executive tried again.

"Great climax—there in the middle—when you stand off the Iroquois all by yourself?"

"Didn't get *that* far yet," said Cooper.

How far *had* he gotten, eager-beaver wanted to know.

[55]

Gary took a look.

"Page 22," he reported.

That wasn't very far, the studio executive suggested, disappointed.

"Nope," said Gary. "But I got so interested, I decided to read it word for word."

He hadn't been that interested in most of the scripts submitted to him of late, for, as he revealed to the Committee, although he had "turned down quite a few scripts because I thought they were tinged with Communistic ideas," he couldn't remember any of their titles.

He was examined by Committee Investigator H. S. Smith.

MR. SMITH: Can you name any of those scripts?

MR. COOPER: No; I can't recall any of those scripts to mind.

MR. SMITH: Can you tell us—

MR. COOPER: The titles.

MR. THOMAS: Just a minute. Mr. Cooper, you haven't got that bad a memory.

MR. COOPER: I beg your pardon, sir?

MR. THOMAS: I say, you haven't got that bad a memory, have you? You must be able to remember some of those scripts you turned down because you thought they were Communist scripts.

MR. COOPER: Well, I can't actually give you a title to any of them; no.

MR. THOMAS: Will you think it over, then, and supply the Committee with a list of those scripts?

MR. COOPER: I don't think I could, because most of. the scripts I read at night, and if they don't look good to me I don't finish them or if I do finish them I send them back as soon as possible to their author.

Chairman Thomas said he understood.

Mr. Cooper told the Committee he "believed he had noticed some Communist influence in Hollywood."

It was spread, he said, through "word of mouth."

MR. THOMAS: Will you speak louder, please, Mr. Cooper.

Mr. Cooper spoke up.

MR. COOPER: Well, I mean sort of social gatherings.

MR. SMITH: That has been your observation.

MR. COOPER: That has been my only observation, yes.

MR. SMITH: Can you tell us some of the statements that you may have heard at these gatherings that you believe are Communistic?

MR. COOPER: Well, I have heard quite a few, I think, from time to time over the years. Well, I have heard tossed around such statements as "Don't you think the Constitution of the United States is about 150 years out of date?" and—oh, I don't know—I have heard people mention that, well, "Perhaps this would be a more efficient Government without a Congress"—which statements I think are very un-American.

He had never had any "personal experience where the Communist Party may have attempted to use you?"

MR. COOPER: They haven't attempted to use me, I don't think, because, apparently, they know that I am not very sympathetic to Communism. Several years ago, when Communism was more of a social chit-chatter in parties, in offices, and so on, when Communism didn't have the implications that it has now, discussion of Communism was more open and I remember hearing statements from some folks to the effect that the Communistic system had a great many features that were desirable, one of which would be desirable to us in the motion picture business in that it offered the actors and artists—in other words, the creative people—a special place in Government where we would be somewhat immune from the ordinary leveling of income. And as I remember, some actor's name was mentioned to me who had a house in Moscow which was very large—he had three cars, and stuff, with his house being quite a bit larger than my house in Beverly Hills at the time—and it looked to me like a pretty phony come-on to us in the picture business. From that time on I could never take any of this pinko mouthing very seriously, because I didn't feel it was on the level.

Mr. Cooper went on to say that he found it "very shocking to hear someone with a lot of money say such a thing as 'The Constitution of the United States is 150 years out of date.'"

[57]

But he had not been solicited to join "the Communist Party or any of its fronts."

He wasn't sure whether Communism in Hollywood was "on the increase or on the decrease."

MR. COOPER: It is very difficult to say right now, within these last few months, because it has become unpopular and a little risky to say too much. You notice the difference. People who were quite easy to express their thoughts before begin to clam up more than they used to.

He had heard of the suggested bill to outlaw the Communist Party in the United States, but hesitated to give it his unqualified approval.

MR. COOPER: I think it would be a good idea, although I have never read Karl Marx and I don't know the basis of Communism, beyond what I have picked up from hearsay. From what I hear, I don't like it because it isn't on the level. So I couldn't possibly answer that question.

There were no more questions. The Chairman thanked Mr. Cooper for coming to Washington, and hoped they hadn't put him out too much.

MR. COOPER: Not at all.

Ronald Reagan, President of the Screen Actors' Guild, and his two predecessors in that office, Robert Montgomery and George Murphy, displayed in their testimony before the House Un-American Activities Committee, a sweet spirit of unanimity.

They chorused that, while there was a militant Communist minority in their Guild, it was very small—Mr. Murphy put the figure at 1 percent of the membership—and had never, "at any time," dominated Guild policy.

There had been no Communist propaganda in any scripts that they, as individuals, had anything to do with, and the industry was "doing a good job of keeping those people's activities curtailed."

Whatever their personal opinions, they felt Government— not actors—should decide whether the Communist Party should be outlawed.

[58]

Mr. Montgomery, after answering "yes, sir" to a series of statements which were apparently the Committee's opinions, was commended for his ability to express himself "articulately, intelligently, and fairly on a matter which is of great interest to this country at the present time."

Mr. Murphy, the Committee's Mr. McDowell said, also had proved a "good witness" for the "fact-finding" inquiry.

"It is very fortunate," he said, "for the American film industry, producers, actors, workers, painters, everybody else, that there has been a group of you fellows out there, men and women, who have had the courage of your convictions, and have stood up and fought. You have done a fine job."

Chairman Thomas, stung by a quote from Thomas Jefferson in Mr. Reagan's testimony to the effect that the American people, acquainted with the facts, would not make a mistake, wanted to get one thing straight.

"That is just why this Committee was created by the House of Representatives," he said, "to acquaint the American people with the facts. Once the American people are acquainted with the facts there is no question but what the American people will do a job, the kind of job that they want done; that is, to make America just as pure as we can possibly make it."

He still thought, Mr. Reagan dared to reply, that democracy could do it.

DEFENSE

IT required a livelier imagination and a deeper pessimism than any of the "unfriendly" witnesses possessed to anticipate the ferocity of that first week of testimony. But in the end, they were inured, even when it was freely urged that they be stripped of their citizenship, deported to foreign countries, or turned over to mobs and lynched.

The witnesses friendly to the Committee may never be called to account at law by those who may have been injured. For their testimony was given under the protective cloak of immunity.

No refutation of charges can ever be expected to achieve the circulation among the American people which the original charges received at the hands of the press.

It is an interesting afternote to the proceedings narrated up to this point, that the friendly witnesses—who so bitterly condemned the others for their refusal to surrender constitutional immunities before the Committee—themselves have consistently refused to surrender their own immunity and submit themselves to civil suits for libel and slander—and to others more serious.

CHAPTER 8

"I would like the opportunity of pointing out to the Committee that it has no legal or constitutional power to proceed."

NOT since the days of the Doges, when the lives and fortunes of Venetian citizens were worth no more than a slip of paper placed in the Lion's Mouth by a bad neighbor, has there been such an orgy of character assassination as during the first phase of these hearings.

Five days and twenty-three witnesses after they began, the Old House Caucus Room was littered with the *disjecta membra* of professional reputations. Shards of broken character lay all about. A review of the testimony up to that point showed that upwards of a hundred men and women, hitherto honorably identified with motion pictures, had been denounced. Professional organizations to which they belonged were characterized as incorporated conspiracies; or at best, as legions of "dupes."

The very climate of Washington was ideal for this carnival of spying and solemn gossip. Not one of the nineteen "unfriendly" witnesses was able to report that he enjoyed a single telephone conversation uninterrupted by strange clickings and occasional voices on the same wire. Waiters hovered too long at tables where these men dined. Sauntering figures took near-by chairs and leaned back to listen better, when the men fled to the lobbies of hotels to consult with their lawyers. An old Washington-hand warned them that microphones bloomed everywhere and it would be better to conduct their conferences in the park behind the Shoreham Hotel.

In this atmosphere, after a long Congressional-type weekend, J. Parnell Thomas resumed the hearings with another mighty whack of the gavel. This time, to nineteen men in the front rows, it sounded like a pole-axe.

[62]

John Howard Lawson who had been named third in the order of witnesses for this day was surprised when he heard himself called to the stand as the first witness. But his attorneys, Robert W. Kenny and Bartley C. Crum, who keep diaries carefully, approached the rostrum first.

"You will recall," said Mr. Kenny, addressing Thomas, "at the outset of this hearing, Mr. Crum and I made a motion to quash the subpoenas addressed to Mr. Lawson and some eighteen other witnesses. . . ."

Thomas appeared not to recall. He wore a puzzled look, as though the presentation of that motion was something far away and long ago. Indeed some hundreds of thousands of words had gushed over the spillway since. But here is what happened:

Before the first witness was sworn on October 20, the same two lawyers had addressed the chairman to inform him that they were prepared to argue a motion to quash the indictments. "It seems to me," Kenny had said, "that the most orderly way to proceed would be to do so before a witness has been sworn. . . . If the Committee is without constitutional authority to proceed to. . . ."

J. Parnell Thomas cut him off, clean, to ask, "What is your name, please?"

That was to show Robert W. Kenny, President of the National Lawyers Guild, former Attorney-General of the State of California and no stranger to Washington, just where he and his associate Bartley C. Crum stood in this hearing room. He invited Mr. Kenny to come back with his motion next week sometime, as though he were an insurance salesman.

MR. KENNY: Mr. Chairman—

MR. THOMAS: That is all.

MR. CRUM: May we ask if we have the right to cross-examine?

MR. THOMAS: You may not ask one more thing at this time. Please be seated.

Now that the week had rolled around, Kenny and Crum were back with their petition. But it had fattened in the week that had passed.

"We think two additional evidences of the illegality of this Committee came out," said Kenny.

He enumerated:

"In attempts by members of the Committee to dictate to various producers the content of films that are to be produced; and:

"An effort indicated by questioning to induce the motion picture producers to create a blacklist, to hire men not on the basis of ability, but on the basis of political beliefs.

"Now both of these, we say, indicate an unconstitutional purpose, a purpose to invade the domain protected by the first amendment, which is the provision that Congress shall pass no law invading the freedom of speech or of conscience."

The earlier motion to quash did not bear the two points which as Kenny claimed, were made imperative by the nature of the hearings. Still, it was a document that gave the Committee pause. In the language of the lawyers, it argued.

One: The motion picture, as a medium of expression, is entitled to the full protection of the First Amendment to the Constitution of the United States in the same way as newspapers and the radio.

Two: The Thomas Committee is attempting to control the content of motion pictures in such a way as to exact national conformity to the views of the Committee.

Three: Congress is without power to censure the thinking and the expression of the American people; and the Committee has attempted to exercise the power of censorship; it is, therefore, an entirely unconstitutional creation without power to compel anyone to appear and testify before it.

Four: The resolution establishing the Committee is void because it authorizes the investigation of "propaganda." It is a term which operates entirely within the realm of opinion, thought, speech, and advocacy—the very thing which is protected by the First Amendment against any legislative restriction. The Committee's power of inquiry is limited by the power of Congress to legislate. Any inquiry not related to a valid legislative purpose is unauthorized and void. Inasmuch as Congress cannot legislate with respect to propaganda, it cannot appoint a committee with the power to inquire into that field.

Five: The very classification of speech into "good" and "bad" speech, into "American" and "Un-American" speech, is itself an abridgment of speech. Speech, whether it is labeled "propaganda" or anything else, cannot be classified as "good" or "bad," "American" or "Un-American" so far as the First Amendment is concerned. It is only when the field of speech or propaganda is passed and the field of action is entered into that the First Amendment no longer stands as a guard against legislative action.

Six: This Committee has characterized the most moderate ideas of social change as subversive and un-American propaganda. It has vilified distinguished persons for daring to disagree with it. The Committee has brought to the American scene the notion of a police state, which is contrary to every basic concept of a democracy.

Seven: The resolution under which the Committee acts is so vague and indefinite as to make it impossible for any person to determine whether a question put to him by the Committee is pertinent to the inquiry. The terms "subversive" and "Un-American" have different meanings according to the point of view of the person using them. A statute using terms so vague and indefinite cannot be the basis for a criminal prosecution.

The amended motion maintained further:

Eight: The entire history of the House Committee on Un-American Activities establishes that it has a non-legislative purpose; that is, that its purpose has been not to obtain information for the purpose of drafting and proposing legislation, but rather that it has been to do such things as interfere in elections, interfere in strikes, attempt directly to control radio, the screen and other media of expression.

Chief Investigator Stripling recognized this document for exactly what it was—an invitation for the Un-American Activities Committee to commit hara-kiri.

"A committee of Congress can no more set aside a law than it can do any other thing," was Stripling's judgment. "I see no point for the Committee to interrupt its proceedings to permit Mr. Kenny to stand up and make a lot of points which he knows are out of order before this tribunal."

MR. KENNY: The Committee is a servant of the Constitution, just as much as the citizen is, and certainly Congress should be given the opportunity, or any committee of Congress, to consider whether or not it is proceeding constitutionally.

The specter of unconstitutionality has not often given legislative bodies pause—not as often, at least as it has stayed the hand of the executive. But here, J. Parnell Thomas pondered.

MR. THOMAS: All right, Mr. Kenny. We have read your brief carefully. In view of the additional points, however, which you bring up, why, the Committee will now take under consideration the whole question, not only based on your original brief, but also these additional points. The Committee will go into executive session until we have concluded.

Here was a question that was of the essence: the life or death of the House Un-American Activities Committee. If life, then the most cogent reasons, the most profound citations would be brought forth. If death—it would have to be by its own hand. Either way, it was a question that could not be decided in the time that it takes to cast dice out of the cup.

The Committee returned in less than twenty minutes.

MR. THOMAS: The meeting will come to order. Mr. Kenny, this is the unanimous decision of this sub-committee. . . . No Committee of Congress has the right to establish its own legality or constitutionality. A committee of Congress cannot disqualify itself from the provisions of the law. We operate under Public Law 601. We cannot set aside this law to suit the convenience of certain witnesses or their counsel. . . . Mr. Stripling, the first witness. . . .

Public Law 601 to which J. Parnell Thomas made reference is on the books in language that is faintly reminiscent of the Alien and Sedition Acts of 1798 and about which Thomas Jefferson later wrote:

"The Federal Courts had subjected certain individuals to its penalties of fine and imprisonment. In coming into office

I released these individuals by the power of pardon . . . which could never be more properly exercised than where citizens were suffering without the authority of law, or, which was equivalent under a law unauthorized by the Constitution, and therefore null."

CHAPTER 9

"I am not on trial here, Mr. Chairman. This Committee is on trial here before the American people. Let us get that straight."

THE germ of the Committee's illegality, which had been incubating for some days, broke out in a rash of self-assertion with overtones of defiance during this second, or defense phase of the hearings. Having cloaked itself in total legality, it was called upon once more to carry out a legal process which the attorneys for the nineteen "unfriendly" witnesses assumed to be a matter of course.

Bartley Crum requested the right to cross examine witnesses, "to bring back Adolphe Menjou, Fred Niblo, Jr., John Charles Moffit, Richard Macauley, Rupert Hughes, Sam Wood, Ayn Rand, James McGuinness—"

MR. THOMAS: The request—
MR. CRUM: Howard Rushmore—
(The chairman pounding gavel)
MR. CRUM: Morrie Ryskind, Oliver Carlson—
MR. THOMAS: The request is denied.
MR. CRUM: In order to show that these witnesses lied.
MR. THOMAS: That request is denied. Mr. Stripling, the first witness.
MR. STRIPLING: John Howard Lawson.

John Howard Lawson's first—and last—request of the Committee was for the same privilege granted Mayer, Warner, and the numerous witnesses who preceded him: the right of making a preliminary statement.

A copy of it was handed up to Thomas, who no more glanced at it than he thrust it away from him, aghast. The other members of the Committee looked just as horrified.

"I don't care to read any more of the statement," Thomas said. "The statement will not be read. I read the first line."

Lawson reminded him, "You have spent one week vilifying me before the American public, and you refuse to allow me to make a statement on my rights as an American citizen."

"I refuse you to make the statement because of the first sentence in your statement," was Thomas' ungrammatical, yet unalterable decision.

Shortly thereafter, the strategy for handling the "unfriendly" witnesses was disclosed by Stripling. Two key questions were to be asked. Anything else was just chaff—marking time. They were:

Are you a member of the Screen Writers' Guild?
Are you now, or have you ever been a member of the Communist Party of the United States?

In due time, when the Committee warmed to its work, J. Parnell Thomas referred to the second as the $64 question. The first, by that token, could be called the $32 question.

Lawson's answer to the first question was:

The raising of any question here in regard to membership, political beliefs or affiliation is absolutely beyond the powers of this Committee.

There was applause for this response. Stripling requested that the witness be instructed to be "more responsive."

MR. THOMAS: I think the witness will be more responsive to the questions.

If Thomas meant that Lawson would respond in terms of yes and no, he was mistaken.

MR. LAWSON: Mr. Chairman, you permitted—
MR. THOMAS: (pounding gavel) Never mind—
MR. LAWSON: (continuing)—witness in this room to make answers of three or four or five hundred words to questions here. . . . I am not on trial here, Mr. Chairman. This Committee is on trial before the American people. Let us get that straight.

[69]

It was plain that Lawson was not going to be a push-over. He maintained that he would frame his answers in his own way and not in the Committee's. "My rights as an American citizen are no less than the responsibilities of this Committee of Congress," he said.

Mr. Thomas: Mr. Lawson, you will have to stop or you will leave the witness stand. And you will leave the witness stand because you are in contempt. That is why you will leave the witness stand. And if you are just trying to force me to put you in contempt, you won't have to try much harder. You know what has happened to a lot of people that have been in contempt of this Committee this year, don't you?

Mr. Lawson: I am glad you have made it perfectly clear that you are going to threaten and intimidate the witnesses, Mr. Chairman.

(The Chairman pounding gavel)

Mr. Lawson: I am an American and I am not at all easy to intimidate, and don't think I am.

There followed a number of questions by Stripling as to Lawson's work in films, and then, coldly and incisively:

Mr. Lawson, are you now, or have you ever been a member of the Communist Party of the United States?

"The question of Communism is in no way related to this inquiry, which is an attempt to get control of the screen and to invade the basic rights of American citizens in all fields."

There they had it. Representative McDowell spluttered, "Now, I must object." Thomas pounded his gavel and continued pounding it for the duration of Lawson's reply, not all of which was audible to the spectators, but the sharp ear of the official reporter caught it.

"The question here," Lawson continued over Thomas' gavel-tattoo, "relates not only to the question of my membership in any political organization, but this Committee is attempting to establish the right which has been historically denied to any committee of this sort, to invade the rights and privileges and immunity of American citizens, whether they be Protestant,

Methodist, Jewish, or Catholic; whether they be Republicans, Democrats, or anything else."

There was no longer any wonder as to why John Howard Lawson and the men who were to follow him on the stand were dubbed "unfriendly" by the Thomas Committee.

Thomas tried again with a tone of sweet reasonableness:

MR. THOMAS: Mr. Lawson, the most pertinent question we can ask is whether or not you have ever been a member of the Communist Party. Now, do you care to answer that question?

Lawson replied with a forthright charge that the Committee's aim was to "smear the motion picture industry . . . proceed to the press, to any form of communication in this country. . . . The Bill of Rights was established precisely to prevent the operation of any committee which would invade the basic rights of Americans."

Stripling complained, "Mr. Chairman, the witness is not answering the question."

MR. THOMAS: We are going to get the answer to that question if we have to stay here for a week. Are you a member of the Communist Party, or have you ever been a member of the Communist Party?

MR. LAWSON: It is unfortunate and tragic that I have to teach this committee the basic principles of American—

He was choked off at the last syllable by the gavel and Thomas' repetition of the $64 question. The Chairman decided not to wait a week.

MR. THOMAS: Stand away from the stand. . . . Officers, take this man away from the stand.

(applause and boos)

Capitol police scurried from all parts of the Caucus Room and converged upon Lawson.

Stripling was ordered to proceed. His desk was high with documents pertaining to Lawson. "I have here, Mr. Chairman, over one hundred exhibits showing Mr. Lawson's affiliations with the party," he said.

Stripling began reading manfully, but when he reached the

[71]

third of thirty-five lengthy paragraphs, he said, "Mr. Chairman, would it be agreeable if Mr. Gaston (an assistant) read the remainder of this memorandum? It is single-spaced, nine pages, and if I have to question additional witnesses today it is going to be quite a burden on my voice."

Thus, without objection, there went into the record of the proceedings of the Thomas Committee, to be forever embalmed in the archives of Congress, a monumental catalog of charges to which John Howard Lawson was given no opportunity to reply.

That massive bill of particulars which the Thomas Committee had gathered on Lawson documented such highly treasonable acts as authorship of a standard treatise on the art of playwriting; the writing of a number of stage successes and an even larger number of screen hits. As for his political character, he was accused of being against the election of Thomas E. Dewey and for the Wagner Act. Against lynching and of advocating the third and fourth terms for Franklin D. Roosevelt.

Definitely pinned on him was membership in organizations designed to protect the rights of organized labor and minorities. He had spoken in favor of the Fair Employmet Practices Act and against the poll tax. And on numerous occasions he had actually written political articles. But he had chosen such publications as the *New Masses* and the *Daily Worker* among others wherein to publish his "subversion."

To a greater or lesser degree, dossiers containing similar charges against the remainder of the "unfriendlies" were read into the record in their turn.

Hence, in an effort to balance the books, John Howard Lawson's declaration to the Committee, rejected because the chairman didn't like its first sentence, is set down here:

For a week, this Committee has conducted an illegal and indecent trial of American citizens, whom the Committee has selected to be publicly pilloried and smeared. I am not here to defend myself, or to answer the agglomeration of falsehoods that has been heaped upon me. I believe lawyers describe this material, rather mildly, as "hearsay evidence." To the American public, it has a shorter name: dirt.

Rational people don't argue with dirt. I feel like a man who has had truck-loads of filth heaped upon him; I am now asked to struggle to my feet and talk while more truck-loads pour more filth around my head.

No, you don't argue with dirt. But you try to find out where it comes from. And to stop the evil deluge before it buries you—and others. The immediate source is obvious. The so-called "evidence" comes from a parade of stool-pigeons, neurotics, publicity-seeking clowns, Gestapo agents, paid informers, and a few ignorant and frightened Hollywood artists. I am not going to discuss this perjured testimony. Let these people live with their consciences, with the knowledge that they have violated their country's most sacred principles.

These individuals are not important. As an individual, I am not important. The obvious fact that the Committee is trying to destroy me personally and professionally, to deprive me of my livelihood and what is far dearer to me—my honor as an American—gains significance only because it opens the way to similar destruction of any citizen whom the Committee selects for annihilation.

I am not going to touch on the gross violation of the Constitution of the United States, and especially of its First and Fifth Amendments, that is taking place here. The proof is so overwhelming that it needs no elaboration. The Un-American Activities Committee stands convicted in the court of public opinion.

I want to speak here as a writer and a citizen.

It is not surprising that writers and artists are selected for this indecent smear. Writers, artists, scientists, educators, are always the first victims of attack by those who hate democracy. The writer has a special responsibility to serve democracy, to further the free exchange of ideas. I am proud to be singled out for attack by men who are obviously—by their own admission on the record—out to stifle ideas and censor communication.

I want to speak of a writer's integrity—the integrity and professional ethics that have been so irresponsibly impugned at these hearings. In its illegal attempt to establish a political dictatorship over the motion picture industry, the Committee has tried to justify its probing into the thought and conscience of individuals on the ground that these individuals insert allegedly "subversive" lines or scenes in motion pictures. From the viewpoint of the motion picture producer, this charge is a fantasy out of the Arabian Nights. But it is also a sweeping indictment of the writer's integrity and professional conduct. When I am employed to write a motion picture, my whole purpose is to make it a vital, entertaining creative portrayal of the segment of life with which it deals. Many problems arise in writing a picture. Like all honest writers, I never write a line or develop a situation, without fully discussing its implications, its meaning, its tendency, with the men in charge of production. Where a line or a situation might relate to controversial issues, I am particularly insistent on full discussion, because such issues affect studio policy, critical response and popularity of the picture.

My political and social views are well known. My deep faith in the motion picture as a popular art is also well known. I don't "sneak ideas" into pictures. I never make a contract to write a picture unless I am convinced that it serves democracy and the interests of the American people. I will never permit what I write and think to be subject to the orders of self-appointed dictators, ambitious politicians, thought-control gestapos, or any other form of censorship this Un-American Committee may attempt to devise. My freedom to speak and write is not for sale in return for a card signed by J. Parnell Thomas saying "O.K. for employment until further notice."

Pictures written by me have been seen and approved by millions of Americans. A subpoena for me is a subpoena for all those who have enjoyed these pictures and recognized them as an honest portrayal of our American life.

Thus, my integrity as a writer is obviously an integral part of my integrity as a citizen. As a citizen I am not alone here. I am not only one of nineteen men who have been subpoenaed. I am forced to appear here as a representative of one hundred and thirty million Americans because the illegal conduct of this Committee has linked me with every citizen. If I can be destroyed no American is safe. You can subpoena a farmer in a field, a lumberjack in the woods, a worker at a machine, a doctor in his office—you can deprive them of a livelihood, deprive them of their honor as Americans.

Let no one think that this is an idle or thoughtless statement. This is the course that the Un-American Activities Committee has charted. Millions of Americans who may as yet be unconscious of what may be in store for them will find that the warning I speak today is literally fulfilled. No American will be safe if the Committee is not stopped in its illegal enterprise.

I am like most Americans in resenting interference with my conscience and belief. I am like most Americans in insisting on my right to serve my country in the way that seems to me most helpful and effective. I am like most Americans in feeling that loyalty to the United States and pride in its traditions is the guiding principle of my life. I am like most Americans in believing that divided loyalty—which is another word for treason—is the most despicable crime of which any man or woman can be accused.

It is my profound conviction that it is precisely because I hold these beliefs that I have been hailed before this illegal court. These are the beliefs that the so-called Un-American Activities Committee is seeking to root out in order to subvert orderly government and establish an autocratic dictatorship.

I am not suggesting that J. Parnell Thomas aspires to be the man on horseback. He is a petty politician, serving more powerful forces. Those forces are trying to introduce fascism in this country. They know that the only way to trick the American people into abandoning their rights and liberties is to manufacture an imaginary danger, to frighten the people into accepting repressive laws which are supposedly for their protection.

To anyone familiar with history the pattern for the seizure of dictatorial power is well known. Manufactured charges against "reds," "communists," "enemies of law and order" have been made repeatedly over the centuries. In every case, from the Star Chamber in Stuart England to the burning of the Reichstag in Nazi Germany, the charges have included everyone with democratic sympathies; in every case the charges have been proven false; in every case, the charges have been used to cover an arbitrary seizure of power.

In the terrible wave of repression that swept England at the end of the eighteenth century, Charles James Fox asked a simple question: "We have seen and heard of revolutions in other states. Were they owing to the freedom of popular opinions? Were they owing to the facility of popular meetings? No, sir, they were owing to the reverse of these." The writers and thinkers who were jailed and silenced at that time were all cleared a few years later. The great scientist, Priestley, whose home was burned, was forced to flee to America where

[75]

he was honored as an apostle of liberty. The persecutions under the Alien and Sedition Acts in our own country in 1798 were all proved to be the irresponsible means by which a reactionary political party sought to maintain itself in power. Congress officially repaid all the fines collected under the Sedition Act. The cry of sedition was again raised through the land in 1919 in order to build up the illusion of a non-existent national emergency and thus justify wholesale violations of the Bill of Rights, designed solely to crush labor, prevent American participation in the League of Nations, and keep reaction in power.

Today, we face a serious crisis in the determination of national policy. The only way to solve that crisis is by free discussion. Americans must know the facts. The only plot against American safety is the plot to conceal facts. I am plastered with mud because I happen to be an American who expresses opinions that the House Un-American Activities Committee does not like. But my opinions are not an issue in this case. The issue is my right to have opinions. The Committee's logic is obviously: Lawson's opinions are properly subject to censorship; he writes for the motion picture industry, so the industry is properly subject to censorship; the industry makes pictures for the American people, so the minds of the people must be censored and controlled.

Why? What are J. Parnell Thomas and the Un-American interests he serves, afraid of? They're afraid of the American people. They don't want to muzzle me. They want to muzzle public opinion. They want to muzzle the great Voice of democracy. Because they're conspiring against the American way of life. They want to cut living standards, introduce an economy of poverty, wipe out labor's rights, attack Negroes, Jews, and other minorities, drive us into a disastrous and unnecessary war.

The struggle between thought-control and freedom of expression is the struggle between the people and a greedy unpatriotic minority which hates and fears the people. I wish to present as an integral part of this statement, a paper which I read at a Conference on Thought Control in the United States held in Hollywood on July 9th to 13th. The paper presents the historical background of the threatening situation that we face today, and shows that the attack on freedom of communication is, and has always been, an attack on the American people.

[76]

The American people will know how to answer that attack. They will rally, as they have always rallied, to protect their birthright.

Shortly before noon on the morning of October 27, 1947, J. Parnell Thomas, tapped his gavel ending the drone of a committee investigator who was then on the ninth and last "single-spaced" page of the long, disjointed dossier on Lawson's political life.

MR. THOMAS: Will the investigator suspend for just a minute?
John Howard Lawson refused to answer the question, "Are you a member of the Communist Party? and other questions put to him. Therefore, it is the unanimous opinion of this subcommittee that John Howard Lawson is in contempt of Congress.
Therefore, this subcommittee recommends to the full committee that John Howard Lawson be cited for contempt of Congress and that appropriate resolutions be referred to the House of Representatives.

There was a faint patter of applause from a corner of the spectators' section—the same quarter where earlier was heard in a sort of ventriloquial croak the word "Jew!"
A few minutes later there was another mild demonstration. This happened during an exchange between Eric Johnston and Representative Vail, of Illinois. This discussion was about state and local censorship of films. Some pictures, Vail suggested, are rejected.

MR. JOHNSON: We have had them rejected, like the one in Memphis because it showed a colored boy in the picture with some white boys.
MR. VAIL: He wasn't in the wood pile?

"No," said Johnston, "nor under a chip." But the hissing from the audience drowned that out.

CHAPTER 10

> *"I shall answer in my own words. Very many
> questions can be answered 'Yes' or 'No' only by
> a moron or a slave."*

IF the Thomas Committee found John Howard Lawson a man
not easily cowed, they discovered in Dalton Trumbo a veritable
ring-tailed tiger. He had come to the hearing room that morning
with a large box bulging with motion picture scripts. Under his
chair were several tins containing sixteen-millimeter prints of
pictures he had written.

He explained why he had them: Jack Warner had brought
in a bale of testimonials concerning the magnificent work of
Warner Brothers and his own share in it. Louis B. Mayer had
done likewise to a degree that was almost immodest. And since
a number of "friendly" witnesses had impugned Trumbo's work
and his character, he brought some samples of it to show the
Committee, that they may judge if Trumbo was just a bum or
an honest craftsman. But first, he had a simple request to make
of the Committee—

May I request of the Chair the opportunity to read a statement into
the record?

MR. THOMAS: May we see your statement? . . . to determine
whether it is pertinent to the inquiry.

Mr. Stripling asked for a copy which was furnished him, all
very polite, and for a few minutes they read. Then:

MR. THOMAS: The Chair is ready to rule. . . . We have read your
statement here. We have concluded, and unanimously so that this
statement is not pertinent to the inquiry. Therefore the Chair will
rule that the statement will not be read.

MR. TRUMBO: The Chair has considered a statement from Gerald
L. K. Smith to be pertinent to its inquiries.

[78]

The rosy haze of politeness vanished instantly. "That statement is out of order," Thomas snapped.

Trumbo maintained his calm and asked politely wherein his statement was different from that of Smith.

Thomas' reply was to warn Trumbo that if he conducts himself like the first witness yesterday (Lawson) the privilege of testifying before the Committee would be withdrawn from him. But Trumbo continued curious.

MR. TRUMBO: I would like to know what it is in my statement that this Committee fears to read to the American people?

MR. THOMAS: Go ahead, Mr. Stripling. Ask a question. . . . Ask one question, Mr. Stripling.

The $32 question pertaining to Trumbo's membership in the Screen Writers' Guild was propounded. Trumbo demanded at that point to introduce testimony concerning his work and character. Thomas pounded the gavel so loudly that he lost track of the question.

MR. THOMAS: Just a moment. The Chair wants to find out what the question was and to see whether your answer is pertinent to the question. What was the question?

Stripling instead delivered a homily on the conduct of the witnesses.

MR. STRIPLING: Mr. Trumbo, I shall ask various questions, all of which can be answered "Yes" or "No." If you want to give an explanation after you have made that answer, I feel sure that the Committee will agree to that. . . .

MR. TRUMBO: I understand, Mr. Stripling. However, your job is to ask questions and mine is to answer them. I shall answer "Yes" or "No" if I please to answer. I shall answer in my own words. Very many questions can be answered "Yes" or "No" only by a moron or a slave.

Trumbo had evidently scored there. Thomas agreed that "yes" or "no" answers need not be given, and was politely thanked for this indulgence. Trumbo then attempted to intro-

[79]

duce examples of his work, a matter of twenty motion picture scripts, each of which ran anywhere from 115 to 170 pages.

"Too many pages," said Thomas, and Stripling made another attempt to get a "yes" or "no" on Trumbo's membership in the Screen Writers' Guild.

MR. TRUMBO: Mr. Stripling, the rights of American labor to inviolably secret membership have been won in this country by a great cost of blood and a great cost in terms of hunger. These rights have become an American tradition. Over the Voice of America we have broadcast to the entire world the freedom of our labor.

MR. THOMAS: Are you answering the question or are you making another speech? . . . Because if you want to make a speech we can find a corner right up here where you can make some of these speeches.

Trumbo said that he would be willing to do that too. But as to the specific question of his membership in a collective bargaining agency, that was out on a yes-or-no basis.

MR. TRUMBO: You asked me a question which would permit you to haul every union member in the United States up here to identify himself as a union member, to subject him to future intimidation and coercion. This, I believe is an unconstitutional question.

MR. THOMAS: Now, are you making another speech, or is that the answer? . . . Well, can't you answer . . . by saying "Yes" or "No," or "I think so," or "Maybe," or something like that?

MR. TRUMBO: Mr. Chairman, I should like to accommodate you. May I try to answer the question again?

Thomas would have done well to let the matter lie right there. Instead, he asked for enlightenment and got it. Despite the clashing of the gavel, Trumbo declared himself about the Committee's labor record:

"If there were a committee of Congress, all the members of which had voted in favor of the Taft-Hartley bill, it might be considered that committee was hostile to labor."

Mr. McDowell felt saddened about that challenge and remarked that it is no disgrace, you know to identify oneself as a member of a labor union. "Most of us belong to something."

It fell to J. Parnell Thomas to ask Trumbo for the fourth

time if he was a member of the Screen Writers' Guild and was again informed by the witness that labor organizations have the right to secrecy of their membership lists. Thomas tried a fifth time.

MR. TRUMBO: Mr. Chairman, this question is designed to a specific purpose. First—
MR. THOMAS: (pounding gavel) Do you—
MR. TRUMBO: First, to identify me with the Screen Writers' Guild; secondly, to seek to identify me with the Communist Party and thereby destroy that Guild. . . .

Somebody in the audience said, in a loud whisper, "He's got something!"

Thomas was livid. He pounded the gavel furiously and shouted, "Excuse the witness!" But the calm, calculating chief investigator announced that he wasn't through. Trumbo would not be allowed to descend without being asked the $64 question, "Are you now, or have you ever been a member of the Communist Party?"

MR. TRUMBO: You must have some reason for asking this question.
MR. McDOWELL: Yes, we do.
MR. TRUMBO: You do. I understand that members of the press have been given an alleged Communist Party card belonging to me—is that true?
MR. STRIPLING: That is not true.
MR. THOMAS: You are not asking the question. . . .
MR. TRUMBO: I was.
MR. THOMAS: The chief investigator is asking the questions.

Trumbo begged all of their pardons and Thomas repeated the $64 query, whereupon Trumbo said, "I have the right to be confronted with any evidence that supports that question. I should like to see what you have."

J. Parnell Thomas' face wreathed in one of his infrequent grins. "Oh," he said. "Well, you would! Well, you will, pretty soon."

The official record says there was "laughter and applause."

"The witness is excused," said the Chairman. "Impossible."

[81]

Stripling produced a sheaf of papers. He identified them as "nine pages, single space . . . the affiliations of Mr. Trumbo with the Communist Party." He read the first two, and again to spare his throat, turned the work of chanting the balance of the dossier over to his assistant, Gaston.

As for the statement which Trumbo offered, and which was rejected unanimously by the Un-American Activities Committee, this is it:

Mr. Chairman:

As indicated by news dispatches from foreign countries during the past week, the eyes of the world are focused to-day upon the House Committee on Un-American Acitvities. In every capital city these hearings will be reported. From what happens during the proceedings, the peoples of the earth will learn by precept and example precisely what America means when her strong voice calls out to the community of nations for freedom of the press, freedom of expression, freedom of conscience, the civil rights of men standing accused before government agencies, the vitality and strength of private enterprise, the inviolable right of every American to think as he wishes, to organize and assemble as he pleases, to vote in secret as he chooses.

The quality of our devotion to these principles will be weighed most thoughtfully by all who have been urged to emulate the American way of life. Whether we wish it or not, the Committee and its witnesses appear here before the world as a living test of American democracy in action. By reason of this we have all been committed to a very heavy responsibility.

I shall therefore pass quickly over the hearsay and slander of witnesses classified as friendly to this Committee, as well as over other evidence already established as perjury. I call your attention only briefly to political coincidence that nearly all friendly witnesses summoned by the Committee have violently opposed the ideals of Wendell Willkie and Franklin Roosevelt, while without exception the unfriendly witnesses have supported such ideals. I shall make no comment at all on the petty professional jealousies, the private feuds, the intra-studio conflicts which here have been elevated to the dignity of the record. And only with reluctance and shame do I find it necessary to recall how fulsomely this Committee has complimented witnesses who have proposed that all who disagree with them be deprived of citizenship and handed over to the mercy of mobs.

There are three principal points which I wish to stress in my statement to this Committee:

First: In the course of these hearings your Committee has launched a direct attack upon the constitutional rights of property and of management and of that system which we call private enterprise. You have attempted to compel management to hire and fire at your own dictation, without any regard for rights and agreements already established between management and labor within the motion picture industry. But even beyond this, you have attempted to dictate to industry what kind of product it *shall* make and what kind it shall *not* make.

Let every business man in America clearly understand that if this Committee can usurp the rights of management in *one* industry, it has established the precedent by which it can usurp the rights of management in *all* industries. Modern history reveals many instances abroad where workers in private industry have resolutely defended the rights of management against the encroachments of a corporate state. I am certain they will make such a defense in this country against the attempt with which this Committee is presently engaged.

Second: The Committee in its hearings has consistently attacked the constitutional guarantees of a free press, which encompass the guarantee of a free screen. The American film, as a medium of communication, as a purveyor of ideas, is completely beyond the investigatory powers of this Committee. No committee of the Congress can dictate to the motion picture industry what ideas it shall and shall not incorporate into films, nor can it dictate to the American people what ideas they may and may not see upon the screens of their neighborhood theaters.

But you have not exclusively attacked the principle of a free screen. In the past, you have sought to intimidate workers in the radio industry. And during these hearings you have thanked witnesses who have testified against the theater, the publishing business, and the press itself. This constant attempt to interfere with the rights of every medium of free expression provides the consistent brown thread which binds together all testimony thus far presented by friendly witnesses. It clearly reveals your intention to establish a slave screen, subservient

[83]

to the cultural standards of J. Parnell Thomas and the humanitarian precepts of John E. Rankin.

Third: The Committee throughout its hearing has approved even the grossest attacks upon the right of the artist to express his ideas freely and honestly in his work. Similarly, you have sought testimony attacking his right to function in craft organizations and trade unions for the advancement of his interests. You are now attacking his right to think, and seeking by public inquisition to ferret out his innermost ideas and his most private and personal convictions. No institution on earth possesses this power over American citizens. You violate the most elementary principles of constitutional guarantees when you require anyone to parade for your approval his opinions upon race, religion, politics, or any other matter.

We must furthermore remember always that the defense of constitutional rights is not simply a convenience to be invoked in time of need, but a clear and continuous obligation imposed equally upon all of us at all times. We are, as citizens, literally commanded by its implications to defend the Constitution against even the slightest encroachment upon the protective barrier it interposes between the private citizen on one hand and the inquisitors of government on the other.

Already the gentlemen of this Committee and others of like disposition have produced in this capital city a political atmosphere which is acrid with fear and repression; a community in which anti-Semitism finds safe refuge behind secret tests of loyalty; a city in which no union leader can trust his telephone; a city in which old friends hesitate to recognize one another in public places; a city in which men and women who dissent even slightly from the orthodoxy you seek to impose, speak with confidence only in moving cars and in the open air. You have produced a capital city on the eve of its Reichstag fire. For those who remember German history in the autumn of 1932 there is the smell of smoke in this very room.

Dalton Trumbo was in the hearing room, engrossed in the testimony of a Committee investigator, Louis J. Russell. Russell told of obtaining a "Communist Party Registration Card" bearing the name "Dalt T."

"At the time," Russell continued, "I also obtained a code

which reflects the name 'Dalt T' was the name used for Dalton Trumbo. . . .".

Electrifying! It was all that the Committee needed!

MR. THOMAS: The evidence presented before this Committee concerning Dalton Trumbo clearly indicates that he is an active Communist Party member. Also the fact that he followed the usual Communist line of not responding to questions of the Committee is definite proof that he is a member of the Communist Party. Therefore, by unanimous vote of the members present, the subcommittee recommends to the full committee that Dalton Trumbo be cited for contempt of Congress, and that for his refusal to answer the pertinent question "Are you a member of the Communist Party?" and his refusal to answer other questions, the Committee recommends appropriate action be taken by the full committee without delay.

CHAPTER 11

"The American people are going to have to choose between the Bill of Rights and the Thomas Committee. They cannot have both."

IT was next to impossible for any witness before these hearings to lose his audience. But one man brought it off. He was Roy M. Brewer, head of the International Alliance of Theatrical Stage Employees, or, in the parlance of trade unionists, the holder of a pie-card.

The Committee expected much from him. And much he gave. For two hours he ravished the ears with a narrative of how "the Commies" had made a "definite attempt to take over the entire structure of the trade union movement in the studios."

The working press began to doodle on their copy paper; the radio orators filled in with background patter and the newsreel cameramen went out for short beers.

Things didn't perk up until Paul V. McNutt came to the stand. He must have detected an attempt on the part of Thomas to embarrass him by insisting that McNutt try to name from memory all the film studios which he represented. He could name only five.

His errand here was to correct Thomas' implication that the Motion Picture Association had tried by any but fair means to represent its position. But now, his pride injured, he pulled out all the stops.

"We cannot stand by and allow these vicious charges to go unchallenged before the public," he said. "In the Chairman's own words, we were accused of trying to get the Committee to 'lay off' the investigation. . . . Does the Committee have any proof of these gratuitous insinuations? . . . The Committee has stated it intends to conduct a fair hearing and give the American public all the facts. Insinuations and innuendo are never fair and are not facts."

In all, he gave the Committee a thorough raking over. Everybody considered it doubtful if any other witness would be given a chance to talk to it this way.

Abruptly, Albert Maltz, the third of the "unfriendly" witnesses was ordered to the stand.

"It looks bad for this one," several reporters agreed.

Maltz, sworn and identified, said, "Mr. Chairman, I would like the privilege of making a statement, please."

MR. THOMAS: May we see it, please?

"Cat-and-mouse stuff," said another newspaperman, unprepared for Maltz' next remark:

May I ask whether you asked Mr. Gerald L. K. Smith to see his statement before you allowed him to read it?

MR. THOMAS: I wasn't chairman at that time.

MR. MALTZ: Nevertheless you were on the Committee, Mr. Thomas, were you not?

MR. THOMAS: I asked him a great many questions, and he had a hard time answering some of them, too.

MR. MALTZ: I am interested in that, but I still would like to know whether he had his statement read before he was permitted to read it.

MR. THOMAS: Well, we will look at yours.

There was a pause while Thomas and his colleagues examined Maltz' statement. Then—

Mr. Maltz, the Committee is unanimous in permitting you to read the statement.

There was a hush. People acted as if they didn't hear right. But Maltz needed no urging. He read:

I am an American and I believe there is no more proud word in the vocabulary of man. I am a novelist and a screen writer and I have produced a certain body of work in the past fifteen years. As with any other writer, what I have written has come from the total fabric of my life—my birth in this land, our schools and games, our atmosphere

[87]

of freedom, our tradition of inquiry, criticism, discussion, tolerance. Whatever I am, America has made me. And I, in turn, possess no loyalty as great as the one I have to this land, to the economic and social welfare of its people, to the perpetuation and development of its democratic way of life.

Now at the age of 39, I am commanded to appear before the House Committee on Un-American Activities. For a full week this Committee has encouraged an assortment of well-rehearsed witnesses to testify that I and others are subversive and un-American. It has refused us the opportunity that any pickpocket receives in a magistrate's court— the right to cross-examine these witnesses, to refute their testimony, to reveal their motives, their history, and who, exactly, they are. Furthermore it grants these witnesses congressional immunity so that we may not sue them for libel for their slanders.

I maintain that this is an evil and vicious procedure; that it is legally unjust and morally indecent—and that it places in danger every other American, since if the rights of any one citizen can be invaded, then the constitutional guaranties of every other American have been subverted and no one is any longer protected from official tyranny.

What is it about me that this Committee wishes to destroy? My writings? Very well, let us refer to them.

My novel, *The Cross and the Arrow,* was issued in a special edition of 140,000 copies by a war-time Government agency, the Armed Services Edition, for American servicemen abroad.

My short stories have been reprinted in over 30 anthologies by as many publishers—all subversive, no doubt.

My film, *The Pride of the Marines,* was premiered in 28 cities at Guadalcanal Day banquets under the auspices of the United States Marine Corps.

Another film, *Destination Tokyo,* was premiered aboard a United States submarine and was adopted by the Navy as an official training film.

My short film, *The House I Live In,* was given a special award by the Academy of Motion Picture Arts and Sciences for its contribution to racial tolerance.

My short story, *The Happiest Man on Earth,* won the 1938 O. Henry Memorial Award for the best American short story.

This, then, is the body of work for which this Committee urges I be blacklisted in the film industry—and tomorrow, if it has its way, in the publishing and magazine fields also.

By cold censorship, if not legislation, I must not be allowed to write. Will this censorship stop with me? Or with the others now singled out for attack? If it requires acceptance of the ideas of this Committee to remain immune from the brand of un-Americanism, then who is ultimately safe from this Committee except members of the Ku Klux Klan?

Why else does this Committee now seek to destroy me and others? Because of our ideas, unquestionably. In 1801, when he was President of the United States, Thomas Jefferson wrote:

Opinion, and the just maintenance of it, shall never be a crime in my view; nor bring injury to the individual.

But a few years ago, in the course of one of the hearings of this Committee, Congressman J. Parnell Thomas said, and I quote from the official transcript:

I just want to say this now, that it seems that the New Deal is working along hand in glove with the Communist Party. The New Deal is either for the Communist Party or it is playing into the hands of the Communist Party.

Very well, then, here is the other reason why I and others have been commanded to appear before this Committee—our ideas. In common with many Americans, I supported the New Deal. In common with many Americans I supported, against Mr. Thomas and Mr. Rankin, the anti-lynching bill. I opposed them in my support of OPA controls and emergency veteran housing and a fair employment practices law. I signed petitions for these measures, joined organizations that advocated them, contributed money, sometimes spoke from public platforms, and I will continue to do so. I will take my philosophy from Thomas Paine, Thomas Jefferson, Abraham Lincoln, and I will not be dictated to or intimidated by men to whom the Ku Klux Klan, as a matter of Committee record, is an acceptable American institution.

I state further that on many questions of public interest my opinions

[89]

as a citizen have not always been in accord with the opinions of the majority. They are not now nor have my opinions ever been fixed and unchanging, nor are they now fixed and unchangeable; but, right or wrong, I claim and I insist upon my right to think freely and to speak freely; to join the Republican Party or the Communist Party, the Democratic or the Prohibition Party; to publish whatever I please; to fix my mind or change my mind, without dictation from anyone; to offer any criticism I think fitting of any public official or policy; to join whatever organizations I please, no matter what certain legislators may think of them. Above all, I challenge the right of this Committee to inquire into my political or religious beliefs, in any manner or degree, and I assert that not only the conduct of this Committee but its very existence are a subversion of the Bill of Rights.

If I were a spokesman for General Franco, I would not be here today. I would rather be here. I would rather die than be a shabby American, groveling before men whose names are Thomas and Rankin, but who now carry out activities in America like those carried out in Germany by Goebbels and Himmler.

The American people are going to have to choose between the Bill of Rights and the Thomas Committee. They cannot have both. One or the other must be abolished in the immediate future.

There was a long silence when Maltz finished. Thomas had to rap his gavel to get Stripling back into action. He asked Maltz the $32 question, almost whispered it.

MR. THOMAS: Louder, Mr. Stripling.

MR. STRIPLING: Are you a member of the Screen Writers' Guild?

MR. MALTZ: Next you are going to ask me what religious group I belong to. . . . Any such question as that is an obvious attempt to invade my rights under the Constitution.

Asked again, Maltz repeated his conviction that the question was improper. Likewise the $64 question.

MR. THOMAS: Excuse the witness. No more questions. Typical Communist line.

Before he allowed Maltz to leave the stand, however, Thomas lost another round. He asked for Robert W. Kenny to take the stand to explain an interview which appeared that day in the Washington *Times Herald*. In it Kenny was quoted as advising his nineteen clients "to invite prosecution by refusing to say whether they are Communists . . . to 'walk the plank.' "

MR. THOMAS: . . . What I would like to know is did you advise your clients, who are to be witnesses here, three of whom have already taken the stand and refused to answer questions—

Kenny tried to interrupt the Chairman, who persisted in demanding to know what advice Kenny gave his clients.

MR. KENNY: You are not a lawyer, Mr. Thomas, and, as I think your counsel, or some one would advise you, that would be highly inappropriate. If there is one thing that is sacred in this country, it is the matter of advice that a counsel gives his clients.

Thomas' protests grew successively weaker. Kenny grew less charitable and said, "Well, Mr. Thomas, I am not here to be lectured by this Committee. I do think it is the highest impropriety to ask a lawyer what advice he gave his client."

Thomas abandoned the spot before it got hotter and ordered the reading into the record of the Committee's dossier on Albert Maltz. This chore again fell to assistant-investigator Gaston. He had read perhaps 1200 words when he was interrupted:

MR. THOMAS: Mr. Gaston, on what page are you now?
MR. GASTON: Page 3
MR. THOMAS: What is the number of the citation?
MR. GASTON: No. 8.
MR. THOMAS: There are 58 citations all told?
MR. GASTON: That is correct, sir.
MR. THOMAS: Unless the Committee has some objection, we will suspend further reading and place it in the record from this point on.

The Committee had no objections and neither did Mr. Gaston, who said, "All right, sir. Fine."

It appeared likely that after the scolding by McNutt, the lesson in privileged communication by Kenny, and the stinging statement by Maltz, Thomas would crack down on the next witness, Alvah Bessie.

Bessie, the fourth of the nineteen "unfriendly" witnesses, said immediately, "Mr. Chairman, I also have a statement I would like to read to this Committee, if you would like to examine it, or would you prefer to have me read it."

"We will be pleased to examine it," said Thomas. But first there was the formality of Bessie's identification, during which the Chairman scanned the statement carefully.

MR. THOMAS: Mr. Bessie, while there is some doubt that your statement is pertinent to the inquiry, as will be very evident when you read it—

MR. BESSIE: I would still like to have permission to read it.

MR. THOMAS: Just a minute. . . . We are just wondering, in order to save time, if you couldn't read the first couple of paragraphs and then let us put it in the record.

The complete statement of Alvah Bessie to the Committee follows:

It is my understanding of the First Amendment to our Constitution that it expressly forbids Congress to pass any law which shall abridge freedom of speech or of opinion. And it is my understanding of the function of Congressional Committees that they are set up by the Congress for the express purpose of inquiring into matter that may lead to the initiation of legislation in the Congress.

Now either the Constitution and its Bill of Rights mean what they say or they do not mean what they say. Either the First Amendment is binding upon Congress and all legislative bodies of our Government, or it means nothing at all. I cannot agree with this so-called Committee in its implied belief that the Bill of Rights means whatever this body chooses it to mean, or is applicable only to those with whose opinions this Committee is in agreement.

I am not in agreement with the opinions, activities, or objectives of this Committee or any Committee remotely resembling it. And since the only legislation this Committee could possibly initiate would automatically abridge freedom of speech and opinion, and would therefore be automatically unconstitutional, I have come to the conclusion, that will eventually be borne out by events, that this body is totally unconstitutional and without power to inquire into anything I think, believe, uphold, and cherish, or anything I have ever written or said, or any organization I have ever joined or failed to join.

As a one-time newspaperman I have been deeply interested in the mounting reaction of disapproval by the press of the nation of the activities of this Committee. When the conservative New York *Herald Tribune* can say ". . . the beliefs of men and women who write for the screen are, like the beliefs of any ordinary men or women, everybody's business but their own, as the Bill of Rights mentions. Neither Mr. Thomas nor the Congress in which he sits is empowered to dictate what Americans shall think . . ." ; and when the *Chicago Times* can say, "Of course, the real object of Chairman Thomas and the reactionary Republican majority of the House Un-American Activities Committee is not primarily to uncover subversive influences in Hollywood. It is to smear New Dealers and whatever their progressive successors may be called . . ."—then it is not difficult to any intelligent person to realize that if this investigation is permitted to achieve its immediate objective it will not hesitate to move on from the motion-picture industry it has emasculated, to the throttling of the press, the radio, the theater, and the book publishers of America. We saw this pattern at work before, in Hitler's Germany, and we understand it thoroughly. The true purpose of this Committee on Un-American Activities is to provide the atmosphere and to act as the spearhead for the really un-American forces preparing a Fascist America.

In calling me from my home this body hopes also to rake over the smoldering embers of the war that was fought in Spain from 1938 to 1939. This body, in all its previous manifestations, is on record as believing that support of the Spanish Republic was and is subversive, un-American, and Communist-inspired. That lie was originally spawned by Hitler and Franco, and the majority of the American people—in fact, the majority of the people of the world—never believed it. And I want it on the record at this point that I not only supported the Spanish Republic but that it was my high privilege and the greatest honor I have ever enjoyed to have been a volunteer soldier in the ranks of its International Brigades throughout 1938. And I shall continue to support the Spanish Republic until the Spanish people in their majesty and power remove Francisco Franco and all his supporters and reestablish the legal government Franco and his Nazi and Italian Fascist soldiers overthrew.

The understanding that led me to fight in Spain for that Republic, and my experience in that war, teach me that this Committee is engaged in precisely the identical activities engaged in by un-Spanish Committees, un-German Committees, and un-Italian Committees which preceded it in every country which eventually succumbed to fascism. I will never aid or abet such a Committee in its patent attempt to foster the sort of intimidation and terror that is the inevitable precursor of a Fascist regime. And I therefore restate my conviction that this body has no legal authority to pry into the mind or activities of any American who believes, as I do, in the Constitution, and who is willing at any time to fight to preserve it—as I fought to preserve it in Spain.

Patly, and with only few preliminary questions, Stripling asked Bessie if he were a member of the Screen Writers' Guild.

MR. BESSIE: This is the same sort of question that was asked of other witnesses. It involves a question of my association.

MR. STRIPLING: Do you refuse to answer the question?

MR. BESSIE: I have not refused . . . but I must answer the question in the only way I know how, and that is, that I believe that such a question violates my right of association and is not properly falling— I do not believe it falls properly within the scope of this Committee's inquiry.

MR. STRIPLING: We will move on the $64 question, Mr. Bessie. Are you now or have you ever been a member of the Communist Party?

Bessie's answer had something Ciceronian about it. "Mr. Stripling and gentlemen of the Committee," he began. "Unless it has been changed since yesterday in our country, we have a secret ballot; and I do not believe this Committee has any more right to inquire into my political affiliations than I believe an election official has the right to go into a voting booth and examine the ballot which has been marked by the voter. General Eisenhower himself has refused to reveal his political affiliations, and what is good enough for General Eisenhower is good enough for me."

Stripling's comment on that was to the effect that the Un-American Committee found that the Communist Party was not a political party, "but is, in fact, the agent of a foreign government" and therefore he would put the $64 question to him again.

The witness maintained that he had answered and suggested that his reply be read back to Stripling.

In the next exchange between Bessie and Stripling there is a sentence, which lawyers agree, will become more and more important as the issue advances in the courts. It was uttered by Stripling:

"Mr. Bessie, there have been charges made before this Committee that you are a Communist."

A number of people who were in the hearing room at the time insist that what Stripling actually said was, "Mr. Bessie, *you are charged* with being a Communist."

However, the official printed record of the proceedings gives the first version and continues:

. . . I didn't notice anywhere in your statement that you denied that charge. You are now being given an opportunity to deny whether or not you are a member of the Communist Party.

The witness continued to stand on the Bill of Rights. Stripling appealed to the Chair to direct that an answer be given. Thomas, pleading in the interests of saving time to "Answer 'yes' or 'no'; or if you don't care to answer it, just say so."

Bessie insisted that he had already given several answers and was accused of "following the same line as these other witnesses . . . which is definitely the Communist line. . . . You are excused. If you want to make a speech, go out here under a big tree."

The business of reading the dossier on Alvah Bessie was undertaken, this time by Benjamin Mandel of the Committee's staff. He reached the ninth point, with twenty-three more to go when the Chairman lost patience and ordered the rest of it into the record unread.

J. Parnell Thomas thereupon announced that by a unanimous vote of the subcommittee, "because of the failure of Mr. Maltz and Mr. Bessie to respond to questions propounded of them,

[95]

recommends to the full committee that Albert Maltz and Alvah Bessie be cited for contempt."

At that moment too a benediction descended upon the Un-American Activities Committee—a telegram—

Congratulations on your splendid courage. Communist rattlesnakes are bent on inoculating the mind of our American Youth. Clean out the rats. You are not injuring our industry. You are helping to keep them American. Bless you.

It was from Leo Carrillo, actor, rancher, and Grand Marshall of Hollywood's Annual Santa Claus Parade.

CHAPTER 12

"Conscience, sir, conscience."

AND on the eighth day, the Committee paused for a moment to mend its political fences.

In a statement submitted by the Chairman, the Committee tried to show that its existence was in response to popular demand, its functioning was in conformance with law, and that its evidence was the result of "the service of trained investigators, all former FBI agents."

Then the Committee awarded itself a laurel wreath. These brave, pure men had not been "swayed, intimidated, or influenced by either Hollywood glamour, pressure groups, threats, ridicule, or high-pressure tactics on the part of the high-paid puppets and apologists for certain elements of the motion picture industry." Thus they dismissed the Committee For the First Amendment whose activity will be described later, and growing public resentment of the procedures and the purposes of the investigation.

The Committee coyly hid behind the skirts of Mrs. Lela Rogers and Ayn Rand, blubbering that this entire investigation was a Hollywood family squabble.

"Prominent Americans, all from the industry, are the ones who leveled the charges; it wasn't the Committee," Thomas said, wiping his hands of the affair.

The very fact that the "unfriendly" witnesses persistently cited the Constitution, and the Bill of Rights, was, to Mr. Thomas *prima facie* evidence that they were foreign agents.

On this high note, Samuel Ornitz was called to the stand.

The statement offered by Ornitz was rejected by Thomas as "clearly out of order" and "just another case of vilification."

Then Mr. Ornitz introduced a subject with which the Committee was not prepared to deal. In response to a question by

[97]

Mr. Stripling about his membership in the Screen Writers' Guild, Mr. Ornitz said, "I wish to reply to that question by saying that this involves a serious question of conscience for me."

MR. THOMAS: Conscience?
MR. ORNITZ: Conscience, sir, conscience.

Mr. Thomas' pounding gavel was silent long enough to permit Mr. Stripling to ask the $64 question, and when it was obvious that Mr. Ornitz' conscience would not betray him, the witness was told to "stand aside," then to "stand away," and Investigator Russell was called to read the bill of particulars on Ornitz into the record.

But Mr. Gaston, as usual, took over in behalf of Stripling and Russell who were saving their voices for bigger things.

The statement Ornitz had been refused permission to make, follows:

I wish to address this Committee as a Jew, because one of its leading members is the outstanding anti-Semite in the Congress and revels in this fact. I refer to John E. Rankin. I refer to this evil because it has been responsible for the systematic and ruthless slaughter of six million of my people. Nor were they alone to die. Thirty million others died, including American boys. It may be redundant to repeat that anti-Semitism and anti-Communism were the number one poison weapon used by Hitler—but still terribly relevant, lest we forget.

In speaking as a Jew, I speak in a deeper sense as an American, as the one who has to take the first blow for my fellow-Americans. For when Constitutional guarantees are overridden, the Jew is the first one to suffer . . . but only the first one. As soon as the Jew is crushed, the others get it. Or haven't we been through this . . . the most horrible of wars to date!

Nor did this evil die with Hitler. He and his emulators like Rankin propagated it well. The current *Fortune Magazine* poll shows that thirty-six percent of the adult American people have become anti-Semitic and twelve percent anti-Catholic. It reveals a more devastating fact, namely, that this anti-Semitic and anti-Catholic feeling tends to run highest where Jews and Catholics are the fewest, in remote

American communities . . . how sad, to be able to hate someone you haven't even seen!

I am struck forcibly by the fact that this Committee has subpoenaed the three men who made *Crossfire*, a powerful attack on anti-Semitism . . . and appalled by the fact that you characterized them as "unfriendly" witnesses before they were heard and thus prejudiced opinion against them.

Is it mere coincidence that you chose to subpoena and characterize as "unfriendly" the men who produced, wrote, directed or acted in the following feature length pictures and short subjects, which attacked anti-Semitism or treated Jews and Negroes sympathetically . . . *Pride of the Marines, The House I Live In, Don't Be a Sucker, None Shall Escape, Of Mice and Men, The Brotherhood of Man, The Commington Story, Freedom Road, Body and Soul, New Orleans, The Master Race,* and *The Jolson Story.*

On the front page of the Washington papers today we find reported that our Attorney General Tom C. Clark feels "humiliated" because the American Negro people have had to appeal to the United Nations for redress against lynching and discrimination, and as a result, Mr. Clark is going to enlarge the civil rights section of the United States Department of Justice.

The eyes of the world are on this Committee. Let them not see that civil rights have become a mockery in America in a Congressional caucus room, of all places!

Your Committee and its so-called "friendly" witnesses have been unable to name a single line . . . let alone a picture, that is un-American or subversive by any stretch of the imagination.

Therefore, I ask as a Jew, based on the record, is bigotry this Committee's yardstick of Americanism and its definition of subversive? Indeed—another member of Congress, Senator Glenn H. Taylor, has described the conduct of your Committee as—"Fascist-minded . . . parallel to those pre-war leaders in Germany, Italy, and Japan." I declare that the record bears him out.

Therefore, I feel that I stand here in the first line of the defense of our Constitution and Freedom. I must not fail—nor for one moment falter before the threat of contempt, which word sounds like the short way of saying concentration camp.

[99]

I am now ready for your questions. I shall answer them conscientiously.

Herbert Biberman, the sixth "unfriendly" witness, was more fortunate than most. He was able to answer at least one question fully, without being interrupted by the ever-complaining gavel of the Chair. When Mr. Stripling asked: "When and where were you born, Mr. Biberman?" Mr. Biberman answered in his clear, full voice: "I was born within a stone's throw of Independence Hall in Philadelphia, on the day when Mr. McKinley was inaugurated as President of the United States, on the second floor of a building at Sixth and South, over a grocery store."

After this response, Mr. Stripling hoped facetiously that Mr. Biberman would be as detailed and specific in all his answers. Mr. Biberman assured him he would. Unfortunately, he was not given a chance to carry out his promise, for the ever-versatile team of Stripling and Thomas had a Gilbert and Sullivan routine to perform.

In response to the standard question of membership in the Screen Writers' Guild, Mr. Biberman started to reply:

MR. BIBERMAN: It has become very clear to me that the real purpose of this investigation—

MR. THOMAS: (pounding gavel) That is not an answer to the question—

MR. BIBERMAN:—is to drive a wedge—

MR THOMAS: (pounding gavel) That is not the question. (Pounding gavel)

MR. BIBERMAN:—into the component parts—

MR. THOMAS: (pounding gavel) Not the question—

MR. BIBERMAN:—of the Motion Picture Industry.

MR. THOMAS: (pounding gavel) Ask him the next question.

MR. BIBERMAN: And by defending my Constitutional rights here, I am defending—

MR. THOMAS: (pounding gavel) Go ahead and ask him the next question.

MR. BIBERMAN:—the right not only of ourselves—

MR. STRIPLING: Are you a member—

[100]

MR. BIBERMAN:—but of the producers and of the American people.
MR. STRIPLING:—of the Communist Party?

There was another exchange of questions, answers and gavel interludes. Once more, Mr. Biberman reiterated his belief that the purpose of the investigation was to disrupt the motion picture industry by invading the rights of individuals and producers to have thoughts and opinions.

In a moment, Mr. Thomas proved Mr. Biberman's accusation, and even went a step further by demanding dictatorially, that the witness answer the questions put to him in the way Mr. Thomas wanted them answered.

MR. BIBERMAN: Mr. Chairman, I would be very suspicious of any answer that came out of my mouth that pleased this Committee.
MR. STRIPLING: I would too.

Chairman Thomas simultaneously exercised his gavel, and his privilege of excusing the witness. His "Take him away," was delivered in the flamboyant style of Gilbert and Sullivan's Lord High Executioner.

Again, Mr. Russell obligingly trotted up to the stand with the Biberman dossier which was, by now, a repetition of a standard pattern.

The prepared statement of Biberman had been, like Ornitz', declared to be "vilification—and therefore not to be read," is none the less printed here:

I have listened to, watched and read the so-called "testimony," at the so-called "hearings," of the so-called "Committee on Un-American Activities," which the English cartoonist Low has characterized as "a 10 cent version of the American Way of Life," for a week.

I do not consider this Committee to be stupid. On the contrary, I consider it to be evil. It is not Communism the House Committee on Un-American Activities fears, but the human mind, reason itself. It is not force and violence this Committee is investigating, but earnest, unceasing citizenship. This Committee is in the course of overthrowing, not Karl Marx, but the constitutional way of American life.

Intimidation and political bullying is and always has been a great evil. Against it, in America, there is and has been, one and only one protection—the fundamental law, the conscience, the mind and the heart of America, embodied in the Constitution of the United States of America and its progressive ten amendments, the Bill of Rights.

Had this Committee on Un-American Activities been born a century and three-quarters ago, there is little doubt it would have voted against the Bill of Rights, and gone down the drain of history with the Tories of that time. But finding the Constitution in existence, and an obstacle in its path, this Committee seeks to undo it, by bullying the American people into surrendering their respect for, and their faith in, this charter of individual freedom.

This Committee, disregarding the individual American's right to choose his thoughts, as least as freely as he chooses his brand of cigarettes—by bullying and intimidation, diverts attention from the Bill of Rights, so that it may erect in its place, "rule by accusation." It must divert attention from the Bill of Rights because it knows it can never erect "rule by accusation" in a country of free, unrestrained, outspoken citizens. It therefore coddles Mr. Adolphe Menjou into this bit of fashionably treacherous advice, "he won't last long if he is labeled a Communist" and thanks him for his assistance in subverting the American concept of the free individual.

The Bill of Rights was not conceived primarily to protect the status-quo. Those who won national independence for the American people understood very well that the status-quo, by virtue of its inherent strength, is always in the very most protected position, well able to attend to its own security. The Bill of Rights was conceived for those who needed it most; those with wider visions than the status-quo ever represents in respect to man's potential. To those who saw farther horizons for America's development, who felt compelled to push beyond its very real accomplishments, who believed in the perfectability of man and his brotherhood—to them was guaranteed by the Bill of Rights, the calm, the security of mind and person, the dignity necessary to expand the American dream by advocating it and pressing for its fullest realization. Against this right to vision and the right to advocate this vision, the Constitution and the Bill of Rights yielded to no other right, the right of way.

But this Committee is now engaged in an attempt to crush this unyieldable right and to put an end to the calm, the security, and the dignity upon which it feeds. This has been attempted often in our country's history, by other groups of officialdom. Such attempts have had their moments, their hours, even their years, but they have never had a single uninterrupted decade in the long life of our Republic and they never will. America will change, but not into its opposite. America will change out of its own growing nature—the self-confidence, the neighborliness, and the non-intimidability of the American people.

As an American I am proud of a fairly long record of discussion and advocacy of social and economic change under the law. Americans have developed a sense of easy access to public forums, of whatever size, and this has accustomed us very naturally to take our feelings, our opinions, and our desires to our fellow citizens constantly and passionately.

I have never been a stand patter. This has always seemed to me a very dull, uncreative and unrewarding frame of mind. My advocacy of this or that issue has often failed of popular acceptance. In the light of developing history, I have sometimes been proven in error, whether of degree or kind, but I have never felt the necessity of apologizing for error, or boasting of success, because I have felt myself bound to my fellow citizens with a single common tie—the hard, slow and patient work necessary if one is to contribute to the correction of social and economic short-comings, and the development of solutions under law.

If I were guilty of acts of force and violence I would never have been called before this Committee. I would be in the courts. And if I were guilty of such acts against this, my country, and this, my people —I should be in the courts, and convicted and condemned.

It is because I have committed *no acts* against my country and my people that I am here. It is because I have been an active citizen that I am here. No slothful, lazy, self-satisfied or cynical citizen is brought here—except those who are in the service of, or in the same bed with, the members of this Committee. I am here because I love, believe in, respect, and have unlimited faith in my fellow citizens. I have been brought here because I believe they will constantly achieve a richer social and economic life under the Constitution, which will eliminate prejudice and inequality in spite of the efforts of this Committee to prevent it. I have been brought here because I believe the American people will not give up the holy struggle for a peaceful world, will not be bullied into an hysterical war. I have been brought here not because I have dreamed these dreams but because I committed the sin of devoting ten years to energetic advocacy of my faith in the American people under our Bill of Rights. For this I have earned the hatred of this Committee, and of this hatred I am especially proud.

Because my professional life and my life as a free man have been so uncensorable by decent standards, this Committee for Un-American Activities, in order to attempt to embarrass and intimidate me, has, without power or authority under the Constitution, been forced to set up a series of categories such as "Foreign Agent," "Subversive," in order to attempt, by use of these scare phrases, to poison the public mind against me, and against the many, many other Americans who with slow, hard and patient persistence have tried to be the most effective citizens their powers permit.

Between this Committee and the nineteen "unfriendly" witnesses there is an impassable gulf. We are the ends opposite of American life. Either this Committee will be abolished or it will abolish the Bill of Rights and the American way of life along with it. This question will not be decided by the Committee or by us but by the American people. *And this decision will be a decision of, by, and for the continuance of popular constitutional government in our country.*

In this hearing I will not merely rely upon the Constitution—I will fight for it and defend it against all possible intimidation.

Here as well, I am a free man—accustomed to slow, hard, patient, and passionate defense of what I believe to be American.

There is a hymn we sing, and teach our children to sing, which scans as follows:

> My country 'tis of thee
> Sweet land of liberty
> Of thee I sing
> Land where our fathers died
> Land of the Pilgrim's pride
> From every mountain side
> Let Freedom ring!

MR. THOMAS: The Chair would like to announce that by unanimous vote of the sub-committee, the sub-committee recommends to the full Committee that Samuel Ornitz and Herbert Biberman be cited for contempt and that appropriate action be taken immediately.

CHAPTER 13

> "*I believe that I could not engage in any conspiracy with you to invade the First Amendment.*"

THE key to why subpoenas were served on Adrian Scott and Edward Dmytryk, respectively producer and director of the film *Crossfire,* was found when Mr. Stripling, the interrogator, inadvertently addressed Mr. Scott as "Mr. Dmytryk."

Supposedly called before the Committee as separate and unrelated individuals, the link between these two gentlemen in the corporate mind of the Committee was made amply clear by Mr. Stripling's slip of the tongue.

Scott and Dmytryk were subpoenaed *because* they produced and directed *Crossfire.* That now celebrated film attacked anti-Semitism in particular and racial hatred and intolerance generally.

Scott's statement, which, naturally, he was not allowed to read, caused the Chairman almost to blow a gasket.

MR. THOMAS: This may not be the worst statement we have received, but it is almost the worst.

MR. SCOTT: May I disagree with the Chairman, please?

The red-faced Mr. Thomas and the wan Mr. Stripling went on to their investigation in their usual fashion. The blue note was provided by the melancholy of the questioning.

Scott, who remained affable throughout, maintained that the only topics concerning himself which appeared to be of interest to the Committee, his union membership and any possible political affiliation, were none of the Committee's business.

For want of a "yes," "no," or "maybe," the Chairman said he was confused. "From your answer I must be terribly dumb . . . but I can't tell whether you are a member or not."

[105]

Mr. Scott, possibly letting his good manners run away with him, replied, "Mr. Thomas, I don't agree with you. I don't think you are. . . ."

Mr. Stripling pressed the $64 question, addressing Mr. Scott as "Mr. Dmytryk."

MR. SCOTT: I believe that question also invades my rights as a citizen. I believe it also invades the First Amendment. I believe that I could not engage in any conspiracy with you to invade the First Amendment.

Mr. Scott was excused. It took the sub-committee practically no time at all to reach the conclusion that he should be cited for contempt. Whether Mr. Scott actually felt contempt for the Committee, as distinguished from what he deemed to be correct behavior in answering its questions may best be judged from the statement which he was not allowed to make:

I do not believe it is necessary for me to raise my voice against the open war now being waged on civil liberties and on a free screen by the Committee on Un-American Activities. Voices more eloquent than mine have spoken.

I wish to speak about another war. I would like to speak about the "cold war" now being waged by the Committee of Un-American Activities against the Jewish and Negro people.

The evidence is clear and incontrovertible.

Edward Dmytryk, who direct Crossfire, and I, who served Crossfire as producer, have extended invitations to the Committee to view this picture. Our invitations were ignored or refused.

We who made this picture are proud of it. We are proud to lend our voices, however small, in the enormous fight now being waged—and yet to be waged—to destroy the un-American practice of anti-Semitism. We detest anti-Semitism. We detest anti-Catholicism. We detest anti-Protestantism. We detest any practice which degrades any minority or any religion or any people.

We expected the Committee to refuse our invitation to see and to discuss Crossfire. We expected them to refuse to discuss measures by which the practice of anti-Semitism could be abolished. To do this would be incompatible with the Committee's bigoted record and bigoted support.

Individually a member of this Committee may protest that he is not anti-Semitic. He may say that some of his best friends are Jews—or even that some of his best constituents are Jews. Or he may say, in protest, that he loves the Negro people; and the Negro people love him—that, in his poll tax district, the colored man knows that he loves him, providing the colored man keeps his place. But despite his protestations of individual innocence, the evidence of the Committee's collective guilt is cynically clear.

Let the committeeman say he is not anti-Semitic. But the rabble rousing anti-Semitic Gerald L. K. Smith publicly approves and supports him.

Let the committeeman say he is not against the colored people. But the anti-Negro Ku Klux Klan and all hate groups love and work for him.

Let the committeeman whisper in the cloak room that he disapproves of the hatemonger, John Rankin of Mississippi. But has he disavowed him publicly? Has he repudiated his racist doctrine? Has he, more important, recommended legislation which would destroy John Rankin's racist doctrines?

Let the committeeman say he is opposed to inhuman treatment of minorities—and bad housing and unsanitary ghettos. But what measures has the committeeman personally recommended to change all this? Where has his hand been evident in assisting minorities to take their rightful place among their fellow men? What has he done to make fair employment practices a reality?

Let the committeeman say he is not anti-Semitic. *But let the record show he does the work of anti-Semites.*

Let the committeeman say he is not anti-Negro. *But let the record show that he does the work of the Ku Klux Klan.*

Today this Committee is engaged in an attempt to destroy nineteen subpoenaed witnesses. The record of these men is clear. They have always stood for issues which are beneficial to the great mass of the American people.

Many times in their films they have presented the Jew and the Negro (and other minorities as well) in unstereotyped terms. They have made it an uncompromising rule in motion pictures to treat all minorities with dignity.

These men oppose and actively work against Gerald L. K. Smith and the Ku Klux Klan and the Black Legion and the Columbians and all kinds and varieties of hate groups.

They not only say they are against minority oppression, they do something about it.

The Committee is now attempting to deprive these nineteen men of jobs, to establish a blacklist. By slander, by vilification, this Committee is attempting to frighten and intimidate these men and their employers; to silence those voices which have spoken out for the Jewish and the Negro people and other people.

The Committee wants these eloquent voices stilled.

This is the cold war now being waged by the Committee on Un-American Activities against minorities. The next phase—total war against minorities—needs no elaboration. History has recorded what has happened in Nazi Germany.

For myself and my colleagues, we will not be intimidated. We will not be frightened. We will not permit our voices to be put into moulds or into concentration camps. We will continue to lend our voices so that fundamental justice will obtain for Jews, Negroes, and for all citizens.

Here is the partial motion picture record of these men in behalf of minorities:

Robert Rossen wrote the anti-lynch picture *They Won't Forget*. His latest picture is *Body and Soul* which treats Negro and Jew with dignity and justice as free men.

Howard Koch wrote *Casablanca* and *In This Our Life*. The Negro is treated honestly as a free man.

Albert Maltz wrote *Pride of the Marines* and *The House I Live In* which was sung by Frank Sinatra. Both pictures exposed anti-Semitism and religious and racial intolerance.

Waldo Salt wrote *The Commington Story* for the OWI. An attack on anti-Semitism.

Ring Lardner, Jr., wrote the *Brotherhood of Man* calling for more understanding among races and religions.

Herbert Biberman produced *New Orleans,* hailed by the Negro press as intelligent treatment of Negroes.

Lewis Milestone directed *Of Mice and Men* in which the Negro was handled with dignity. And, lest we forget, Nazi Storm Troopers stopped the showing of his anti-war film *All Quiet on the Western Front,* in 1931, in Germany.

Lester Cole wrote *None Shall Escape* which exposed Nazi brutality to the Jews.

Richard Collins wrote *Don't Be a Sucker* for the armed services. Subsequently, it was released to the public. It exposed anti-Semitism and kindred hatreds.

Irving Pichel directed *A Medal for Benny,* which treated a Mexican minority with dignity.

Will the American people allow this bigoted Committee to sit in judgment of these men and their records?

The ineffable Louis J. Russell again returned to the stand. He contributed his customary set of allegations, decorating Mr. Scott with a hatful of Communist numbers. As usual nobody on the Committee asked Mr. Russell where he got his information since counsel for Mr. Scott was not permitted to cross-examine.

A little earlier, with reference to the activities of Edward Dmytryk, Russell had been so explicit that the only conclusion to be drawn would be that Mr. Russell had lived, slept, eaten and breathed with the director of *Crossfire* for several years. Yet Mr. Dmytryk claims no acquaintance with Mr. Russell.

Mr. Dmytryk, an American citizen of Canadian birth, a fact evidently noted by J. Parnell Thomas.

In reply to the question which, by now, Mr. Stripling was ripping off as if it were all one word: "Areyounoworhaveyou-everbeenamemberoftheCommunistParty, Mr. Dmytryk?"

Mr. Dmytryk: Well, Mr. Stripling, I think there is a question of constitutional rights involved here. I don't believe that you have—

Thomas interrupted, scornfully and imperiously. "When did you learn about the Constitution? Tell me when you learned about the Constitution!"

Mr. Dmytryk: I will be glad to answer that question, Mr. Chairman. I first learned about the Constitution in high school and again—

Mr. Dmytryk was infrequently allowed to complete a sentence. This time the interruption came from McDowell.

MR. McDOWELL: Let's have the answer to the other question.

MR. DMYTRYK: I was asked when I learned about the Constitution.

MR. STRIPLING: AreyounoworhaveyoueverbeenamemberoftheCommunistParty?

MR. DMYTRYK: All right, gentlemen; if you will keep your questions simple and one at a time, I will be glad to answer.

Mr. Dmytryk asked for the privilege accorded freely to the "friendly" witnesses; the privilege of making a prepared statement. This was, of course, denied him, the Chairman declaring tartly: "The Chair has ruled that the statement is not pertinent at all. The chief investigator will ask questions, and you will please answer them."

MR. DMYTRYK: All right.

MR. STRIPLING: Mr. Dmytryk, are you a member of the Screen Directors' Guild?

MR. DMYTRYK: Mr. Stripling, I feel that these kinds of questions are designed to—

MR. THOMAS: Just a minute. It is not up to you to "feel" what the design is. It is up to you to answer the questions and be responsive to the questions.

During the previous week, Richard Macauley, a "friendly" witness, had been advised by the Committee's investigator: ". . . we would prefer you name only those in the Guild whom you *feel* are Communists."

Before the Thomas Committee the admissibility of "feelings" evidently depended on who had them.

When the Committee had wearied of its attempts to badger Mr. Dmytryk into abandoning his stated position on what he regarded as constitutional guarantees of his civil liberties, he was excused. After this, Russell and Stripling took turns in blanketing Mr. Dmytryk with accusations which, of course, according to the custom obtaining here, he was given no opportunity to refute.

Dmytryk's suppressed statement follows:

It is my firm belief that democracy lives and thrives only on freedom. This country has always fulfilled its destiny most completely when its people, through their representatives, have allowed themselves the greatest exercise of freedom with the law. The dark period in our history have been those in which our freedoms have been suppressed, to however small a degree. Some of that darkness exists into the present day in the continued suppression of certain minorities. In my last few years in Hollywood, I have devoted myself, through pictures such as *Crossfire,* to a fight against these racial suppressions and prejudices. My work speaks for itself. I believe that it speaks clearly enough so that the people of the country and this Committee, which has no right to inquire into my politics or my thinking, can still judge my thoughts and my beliefs by my work, and by my work alone.

The freedom which is so necessary for the fullest development of a democratic nation is also indispensable for the fullest development of any institution within that nation which deals with ideas and ideals. For without the free expression of ideas, both favorable and critical, no nation can long hope to remain free. This principle has been stated many times before, in far better words than mine. It is a shame that it should have to be repeated here before this Committee.

But the intent is clear. This Committee has demanded that the producers "clean their own house," under the supervision of the Committee's members. They will name the names and the producers must make out the blacklist. But where will it end? History is all too clear on procedures of this kind. There is no end. Is a Committee member anti-Semitic? He will force the producers to blacklist men who deplore anti-Semitism. Is a Committee member anti-labor? He will force the producers to blacklist men who are pro-labor. Is a Committee member against low-cost housing? He will force the producers to blacklist men who advocate low-cost housing. And thus, even without special legislation, he will succeed in throttling, both artistically and financially, one of the greatest industries in the United States. For he will have succeeded, through threats and intimidation, in effectively censoring a screen which has just within the last few years begun to emerge from a never-never land into a dim realization of its responsibilities to the people of this nation and of the world. As an added touch of grim humor, this attempt at censorship is being made just at the time when, as has been remarked by every responsible critic in the country, foreign motion pictures are successfully challenging ours largely because of their free, open and honest approach to the problems that beset modern man.

The men who have here been attacked, and countless others in Hollywood who have stood up in their behalf, have behind them a body of work, completely open to inspection, which expresses their point of view. They have always begged for understanding and enlightment. They have also preached the elimination of certain institutions, yes! They have preached the elimination of the institution of poverty, of slums, of disease, of racial intolerance, and of all that bigotry which prevents men from living in peace and understanding, one with another.

If the Committee succeeds in forcing the producers to blacklist these men it can only result in the destruction of the industry in which they are now employed. For the loss of these men will inevitably lead to the squelching of the ideas they represent, and which they have freely exhibited to the people in such pictures as *The Best Years of Our Lives, Pride of the Marines, Crossfire, The Farmer's Daughter,* yes, and even *Margie!* The resulting deterioration in the quality of American pictures cannot fail to result in the eventual extinction of our industry, both as an artistic expression and, just as important, as a successful business enterprise.

I cannot join in this wholesale liquidation of the principle of free expression but, in company with my fellow-workers, must stand against it in the interest of the entire industry.

At this stage, J. Parnell Thomas' declaration of the Committee's attitude to the witnesses Scott and Dmytryk had become quite formalized.

The Chair desires to announce at this time (or, the Chair would like to announce) that the sub-committee recommends to the full committee that the witnesses Adrian Scott and Edward Dmytryk be cited for contempt. . . .

CHAPTER 14

> *"I am saying my understanding as an American. . . ."*
>
> *"Never mind your understanding. . . . Are you or have you ever been. . . ."*

IT is not certain whether J. Parnell Thomas knew, or intended that Thursday, October 30, 1947, would be the last day of his carnival. But that morning he breakfasted well in his suite at the Mayflower Hotel and arrived at the hearing room looking like a man with a delicious secret. His mood was affable and expansive, in a pink sort of way.

He made a bargain with Ring Lardner, Jr., the ninth of the "unfriendly" ten, who like the others asked permission to make a statement. He agreed that Lardner could make his statement *after* his testimony.

But he was displeased first with the screen writer's answer to the question as to his membership in the Screen Writers' Guild. He chided him, "Now, Mr. Lardner, don't do like the others, if I were you, or you will never read your statement."

MR. LARDNER: But I understood you to say that I would be permitted to read the statement, Mr. Chairman.

MR. THOMAS: Yes; after you are finished with the questions and answers. . . . But you certainly haven't answered the questions.

MR. LARDNER: . . . I don't think you qualified in any way your statement that I would be allowed to read this statement.

MR. THOMAS: Then I will qualify it now. If you refuse to answer the questions then you will not read your statement.

Needless to say, Mr. Lardner did not get to read his statement. He was unable to comply with Thomas' demand to:

. . . answer that "yes" or "no." You don't have to go into a long harangue or speech. If you want to make a speech you know where you can go—out there.

Stripling fired the $64 question.

MR. LARDNER: It seems to me that you are trying to discredit the Screen Writers' Guild through me, and the motion picture industry through the Screen Writers' Guild and our whole practice of freedom of expression.

MR. STRIPLING: If you and others are members of the Communist Party, you are the ones who are discrediting the Screen Writers' Guild.

Lardner tried to clarify his point about the purpose behind the question, but the Chairman lost patience and snorted that "any real American would be proud to answer the question, 'Are you or are you not. . . .'"

MR. LARDNER: It depends on the circumstances. I could answer it, but if I did, I would hate myself in the morning.

This remark from Lardner occasioned considerable curiosity among the press. In an interview with Lardner, published in the New York *Herald Tribune,* January 7, 1948, Lardner clarifies:

Like most of my responses, that one was delivered in pieces, though I insist that I make more sense when I speak than Mr. Thomas does, I will concede him a clear superiority in volume and words per minute. In trying to give my reply to the question about Communist Party membership, I started to say, "I could answer the question exactly the way you want, Mr. Chairman—." Thomas broke in with some thoughts which had just occurred to him on the subject of "real Americanism." I waited until he drew a breath, determined to get one complete parsable sentence into the record, if only to justify the efforts of my childhood English teachers. This time I picked up the thought with "I could answer it—," the words "exactly the way you want" being incorporated in the implication.

What I meant, therefore, was that I would subsequently reproach myself if I ever yielded to the Committee's terms entirely. I have always associated the words "I'll hate myself in the morning" with a situation in which a previously chaste woman is succumbing to the indecent blandishment of a scoundrel and very likely launching herself on the road to prostitution. That is the analogy I wished to suggest.

J. Parnell Thomas had been furious before. But when Lardner said, "I'd hate myself in the morning," the Chairman shouted, "Leave the witness chair! Leave the witness chair!"

"I think I am leaving by force," said Lardner, calmly, as Thomas whanged his gavel and called, "Sergeant, take the witness away."

And while the doughty Mr. Gaston spells Investigator Russell in the reading or Lardner's dossier, here is the statement which was offered by Lardner to the Committee:

I wish to speak briefly on two matters which seem to me very pertinent to these proceedings. The first is my own record as it has been impugned by the testimony of some of your witnesses.

My father was a writer in the best tradition of American literature. That tradition is very closely allied to the democratic ideal in American life. Not only I but my three brothers have also been writers. Two of these brothers were killed in separate chapters of the same great struggle to preserve that democratic ideal, one as a member of the Abraham Lincoln Brigade in Spain in 1938, the other as a war correspondent in Germany in 1944. I make no claim to the genius of my father or the courage of my brothers, but I do maintain that everything I have done or written has been in keeping with the spirit that governed their work, their lives, and their deaths.

My principal occupation is that of screen writer, I have contributed to more than a dozen motion pictures, among them *Woman of the Year,* for which I received an Academy Award. *The Cross of Lorraine,* about the anti-fascist movement in France during the war, the screen version of the play *Tomorrow the World,* about the effects of Nazi education, *Cloak and Dagger,* about the heroic work of our Office of Strategic Services, and an animated cartoon called *The Brotherhood of Man,* based on the pamphlet, *The Races of Mankind,* and exposing the myth that any inherent differences exist among people of different skin color and geographical origin. It doesn't matter to me what kind of preposterous documents your investigators produce from unnamed sources describing my affiliations under some such heavily cloaked pseudonym as "Ring L." My record includes no anti-democratic word or act, no spoken or written expression of anti-Semitism, anti-Negro feeling or opposition to American democratic principles as I understand them.

Secondly, about un-American activities in Hollywood. The atmosphere there, where I have lived for the last ten years, is considerably different than that of the small segment of Washington to which I have been exposed in the last ten days. There are a few frightened people there—men like Adolphe Menjou and John C. Moffit throw so many furtive glances over their shoulders that they run a serious risk of dislocation. And we have a certain amount of un-American activity there; anti-Semitism, white supremacy nonsense and other efforts to subvert the democratic idea. Every note exchanged between the Motion Picture Alliance for the Preservation of American Ideals and this Committee contributes to an anti-American purpose. I wish there were a committee qualified and competent to investigate these matters. But compared to what I have seen and heard in this room, Hollywood is a citadel of freedom. Here anti-American sentiments are freely expressed and their spokesmen heartily congratulated. Here there is such fear of the effects of free speech that men are forbidden to read statements and are cut off in mid-sentence lest they expose too much of what is going on here to the public.

What I am most concerned about is the ultimate result that might come from a successful fulfillment of your purpose. On Tuesday, the Chairman said that there was subversive material in motion pictures and proposed that it be prevented in the future by an industry black-list. The motion picture producers have not indicated that they are gullible enough to fall for such a ruse, but if they ever did, the fact that I might be prevented from working at my profession would be of little account. The really important effect would be that the producers themselves would lose control over their pictures, and that the same shackling of education, labor, radio and newspapers would follow. We are already subject in Hollywood to a censorship that makes most pictures empty and childish. Under the kind of censorship which this inquisition threatens, a leading man wouldn't even be able to blurt out the words "I love you" unless he had first secured a notarized affidavit proving she was a pure white, Protestant gentile of old Confederate stock.

All in six minutes and thirty seconds, Lester Cole, the tenth of the "unfriendly" witnesses was put through the Committee's wringer. The questions snapped like firecrackers. Cole's answers were cautious. He too had a statement to make. It was handed up and Thomas accepted it as though it were an examination paper.

Representative McDowell of Pennsylvania, who reads rapidly, snorted, "I think it is insulting, myself."

The Chairman's verdict was, "Clearly another case of vilification . . . not pertinent . . . will not be read. . . . Mr. Stripling, ask the first question."

It was, naturally, concerning Cole's membership in the Screen Writers' Guild. Cole, like the others had no flat "yes" or "no" for the Committee. He wished to answer in his way.

MR. THOMAS: No, no, no, no, no.

MR. COLE: I hear you, Mr. Chairman, I hear you. . . .

MR. THOMAS: You will hear some more. . . . It is a very simple question.

MR. COLE: What I have to say is a very simple answer.

MR. THOMAS: Yes, but answer it "yes" or "no."

MR. COLE: It isn't necessarily that simple.

"Haven't I the right accorded to me, as it was to Mr. McGuinness and other people who came here?" Cole asked. Evidently not. Stripling grew impatient. The $64 question was put.

MR. COLE: I believe the reason that question is being asked is that there is an election in the Screen Writers' Guild in Hollywood that for 15 years Mr. McGuinness and others. . . .

MR. THOMAS: I didn't even know there was an election out there.

MR. COLE: If you don't know there is an election out there then you didn't hear Mr. Lavery's testimony yesterday.

(Earlier, Emmet Lavery, President of the Guild had testified to the effect that under the constitution of that organization, there were no political means-tests for membership.)

[117]

MR. THOMAS: All right, there is an election there. Now answer the question. Are you a member of the Communist Party?

Cole asked for the right to reply in his own way, "and at times when I feel it is proper."

"We will determine whether it is proper," Thomas said. "You are excused. Next witness, Mr. Stripling."

Stripling's assistant, Louis J. Russell, mounted the stand for the tenth time since the hearings began, to relate his "findings" on Lester Cole.

In a Southern drawl that was by now soporific, he quoted liberally from the *Hollywood Reporter,* the producer-subsidized journal which undertook at times to catechize various writers as to their politics, and failing to get the kind of answers it sought grew progressively more careless in its charges.

Russell mentioned that he had a list of the pictures that Cole had written. It was one of the most impressive in the screen-writing craft, numbering more than 35 feature films.

"We will eliminate mentioning the pictures," said Thomas. But the rest of Cole's dossier was to be chanted lustily.

Cole's preliminary statement, which Thomas also "eliminated mentioning" is here:

I want to say at the outset that I am a loyal American, who upholds the Constitution of my country, who does not advocate force and violence, and who is not an agent of a foreign power.

This Committee has announced many times its interest in facts pertinent to this inquiry. I believe many such facts are embodied in this statement.

I have been a working screen-writer in the Motion Picture Industry since 1932. To date, I have written thirty-six screen plays, the titles of which and companies which produced them are attached.

I was working in Hollywood in 1933 when screen writers, faced with an arbitrary fifty percent cut in salaries, formed the Screen Writers' Guild for the purpose of collective bargaining.

From the very start there were attempts to create strife within the industry by groups who used the same technique employed by this Committee.

After years of failure by James Kevin McGuinness, Rupert Hughes and other of your friendly witnesses to disrupt the Screen Writers' Guild, and with it the industry, a desperate appeal was made to Martin Dies, former Chairman of this Committee. Or maybe Martin Dies made the appeal; at any rate the investigations began.

When the Dies investigation proved unsuccessful because of the united resistance of the men and women of the industry, a new tactic was employed. Willie Bioff and George S. Browne were called into the fray.

These two men, Browne and Bioff who ran the IATSE, the union which was represented here the other day by Mr. Roy Brewer, took on the job of creating chaos in the industry. They bought full page advertisements in the Hollywood trade papers, the *Reporter* and the *Daily Variety,* announcing their intentions of taking over all independent Hollywood Guilds and Unions, but only, of course, for one purpose; the eradication of Communism. You will recall that Al Capone, just before going to jail, called upon the American people to "eradicate" all subversive un-American influences in American life, including Communism. By a strange coincidence, the warning of Browne and Bioff also was issued but a short time before they too went to jail for the extortion of huge sums of money; a shakedown of the motion picture industry.

For fifteen years these men have engaged in slander, malicious gossip, near libel; in fact, in every method known to man but one— traditional American democratic procedure.

As in years gone by they accommodated Martin Dies, and later extortionists Browne and Bioff, today McGuinness, Incorporated is playing footsie with the House Committee on Un-American Activities. They think the Committee is stooging for the Motion Picture Alliance; the reverse is true.

From what I have seen and heard at this hearing, the House Committee on Un-American Activities is out to accomplish one thing, and one thing only, as far as the American Motion Picture Industry is concerned; they are going either to rule it, or ruin it.

This Committee is determined to sow fear of blacklists; to intimidate management, to destroy democratic guilds and unions by interference in their internal affairs, and through their destruction bring chaos and strife to an industry which seeks only democratic methods with which

[119]

to solve its own problems. This Committee is waging a cold war on democracy.

I know the people in the motion picture industry will not let them get away with it.

Without leaving the rostrum, J. Parnell Thomas and his colleagues, with nods and looks concurred in a recommendation that Lester Cole and Ring Lardner, Jr., be cited for contempt of Congress.

CHAPTER 15

"Literature has the right and the duty to give to the public the ideas of the time."

IT was just before noon. The tempo of the Committee was being speeded up to match the hectic rhythm pounded out by Chairman Thomas' gavel. Everything, this Thursday morning, had to be quickly out and rapidly dried, for Mr. Thomas had promised a world-shaking revelation, and the world did not want to wait. Ever the keen judge of a headline, he had pro-advertised his product, and pre-sold his audience without once giving away his cast or his story. His teaser-campaign had for its theme: "Who Is the Mystery Witness? or, You Ain't Heard Nothin' Yet!" The reporters, all save those who worked for the Hearst press, and who knew more than their headlines let on, were waiting to flash the bulletin. Even the "unfriendly witnesses" were caught in the mounting tension of excitement. Who, indeed, was the Committee's Mystery Witness, and what earth-heaving disclosures would he make?

There was time for one more citation before lunch. He looked easy—a mild, middle-aged, Middle-European.

Up to now, the Committee had been like a stock-company displaying its protean repertory. Extremely versatile, they had managed to perform everything from cloak-and-dagger to light opera. And now, they had before them an opportunity to put on a comic after-piece.

Mr. Brecht had an accent, a soft, broad German accent. Mr. Thomas and Mr. Stripling played their roles as straight men very well. They were over-polite, over-cautious, over-solicitous, and decidedly overboard in their exaggerated attempts to garner a few laughs at the expense of Mr. Brecht's deliberate English.

MR. STRIPLING: Mr. Brecht, will you please state your full name and present address for the record, please? Speak into the microphone.

MR. BRECHT: My name is Berthold Brecht. I am living at 34 West Seventy-third Street, New York. I was born in Augsburg, Germany, February 10, 1898.

MR. STRIPLING: Mr. Brecht, the Committee has a—

MR. THOMAS: What was that date again?

MR. STRIPLING: Would you give the date again?

MR. THOMAS: Tenth of February, 1898.

MR. McDOWELL: 1898?

MR. BRECHT: 1898.

MR. STRIPLING: Mr. Chairman, the Committee has here an interpreter, if you desire the use of an interpreter.

MR. CRUM: Would you like an interpreter?

MR. THOMAS: Do you desire an interpreter?

MR. BRECHT: Yes.

And Mr. Brecht was promptly given an interpreter, a Mr. David Baumgardt, and the joke became twice as good, for Mr. Baumgardt, a consultant of Philosophy at the Library of Congress, like Mr. Brecht, had an accent too—less soft and even broader.

At this point, Chairman Thomas made his best showing as a conscientious Congressman. Tensed as he undoubtedly was by the wonder he was scheduled to unveil that afternoon, and keyed up by the excitement of the expectant audience, nevertheless, he permitted Stripling time to examine every detail with statesmanlike scrupulousness. Scarcely two minutes earlier, Brecht had established his birth date after careful questioning by the Chair, and members of the Committee. But now the question arose again.

MR. STRIPLING: You were born in Augsburg, Bavaria, Germany on February 10, 1888; is that correct?

MR. BRECHT: Yes.

MR. STRIPLING: I am reading from the immigration records—

MR. CRUM: I think, Mr. Stripling, it was 1898.

MR. BRECHT: 1898.

MR. STRIPLING: I beg your pardon.

MR. CRUM: I think the witness tried to say 1898.

MR. STRIPLING: I want to know whether the immigration records are correct on that. Is it '88 or '98?

MR. BRECHT: '98.

Having split this hair accurately, the Committee moved on to weightier matters. They discovered from Brecht's testimony that he left Germany in February 1933 when Hitler took power. He went to Denmark, but when war seemed imminent, in 1939, he moved to Stockholm. When Hitler invaded Norway and Denmark, Brecht left Sweden after one year's residence, and moved again to Finland to await his visa for the United States. He had entered the United States in 1941, and had applied for his first citizenship papers at once.

Brecht was a playwright and a poet by profession. He was currently not employed. His only connection with the Hollywood studios had been through the sale of his story, *Hangmen Also Die* to an independent producer, and through another story that had not yet been produced.

Obviously, there was no point in asking Mr. Brecht the $32 question about membership in the Screen Writers' Guild, Mr. Stripling let him try for $64 at once, and it was at this point, that Brecht asked if•he could read a statement.

After examining the statement, the Chairman failed to blow up as he usually did, but he rejected what Mr. Brecht had written, saying:

Mr. Brecht, the Committee has carefully gone over the statement. It is a very interesting story of German life, but it is not at all pertinent to this inquiry. Therefore, we do not care to have you read the statement.

Perhaps, the Committee honestly could see no connection between the shy little man who was a fugitive from the Gestapo, the sensitive man who had been uprooted from his native land by a relentless Nazism, the man who had been driven three-quarters of the way around the world by fear; and the little man who sat before them, paper in hand. Perhaps, as the Committee said, what had happened in Germany, was an interesting story, but not at all pertinent to the Committee's inquiry. Perhaps.

But the little man's statement spoke for itself.

[123]

I was born in Augsburg, Germany, the son of an industrialist, and studied natural sciences and philosophy at the universities of Munich and Berlin. At the age of twenty, when participating in the war as a member of the medical corps, I wrote a ballad which the Hitler government used fifteen years later as reason for my expatriation. The poem *Der Tote Soldat (The Dead Soldier)* attacked the war and those wanting to prolong it.

I became a playwright. For a time, Germany seemed to be on the path of democracy. There was freedom of speech and of artistic expression.

In the second half of the 1920's, however, the old reactionary militarist forces began to regain strength.

I was then at the height of my career as a playwright, my play *Dreigroschenoper* being produced all over Europe. There were productions of plays of mine at Berlin, Munich, Paris, Vienna, Tokio, Prague, Milano, Kopenhagen, Stockholm, Budapest, Warschau, Helsinki, Moscow, Oslow, Amsterdam, Zurich, Buckarest, Sofia, Brussels, London, New York, Rio de Janeiro, etc. But in Germany voices could already be heard demanding that free artistic expression and free speech should be silenced. Humanist, socialist, even Christian ideas were called "undeutsch" (un-German), a word which I hardly can think of without Hitler's wolfish intonation. At the same time, the cultural and political institutions of the people were violently attacked.

The Weimar Republic, whatever its faults had been, had a powerful slogan, accepted by the best writers and all kinds of artists: *Die Kunst dem Volke (Art Belongs to the People)*. The German workers, their interest in art and literature being very great indeed, formed a highly important part of the general public of readers and theatre-goers. Their sufferings in a devastating depression which more and more threatened their cultural standards, the impudence and growing power of the old militarist, feudal, imperialist gang alarmed us. I started writing some poems, songs and plays reflecting the feelings of the people and attacking their enemies who now openly marched under the swastika of Adolf Hitler.

The persecutions in the field of culture increased gradually. Famous painters, publishers and distinguished magazine editors were persecuted. At the universities, political witch hunts were staged, and cam-

[124]

paigns were waged against motion pictures such as *All Quiet on the Western Front.*

These, of course, were only preparations for more drastic measures still to come. When Hitler seized power, painters were forbidden to paint, publishing houses and film studios were taken over by the Nazi party. But even these strokes against the cultural life of the German people were only the beginning. They were designed and executed as a spiritual preparation for total war which is the total enemy of culture. The war finished it all up. The German people now have to live without roofs over their heads, without sufficient nourishment, without soap, without the very foundations of culture.

At the beginning, only a very few people were capable of seeing the connection between the reactionary restrictions on the field of culture and the ultimate assaults upon the physical life of a people itself. The efforts of the democratic, anti-militarist forces, of which those in the cultural field were, of course, only a modest part, then proved to be weak altogether; Hitler took over. I had to leave Germany in February, 1933, the day after the Reichstag fire. A veritable exodus of writers and artists began of a kind such as the world had never seen before. . . . I settled down in Denmark and dedicated my total literary production from that time on to the fight against Naziism, writing plays and poetry.

Some poems were smuggled into the Third Reich, and Danish Naziism supported by Hitler's embassy, soon began to demand my deportation. Of course, the Danish government refused. But in 1939 when war seemed imminent, I left with my family for Sweden, invited by Swedish senators and the Lord Mayor of Stockholm. I could remain only one year. Hitler invaded Denmark and Norway.

We continued our flight northward, to Finland, there to wait for immigration visas to the U.S.A. Hitler's troops followed. Finland was full of Nazi divisions when we left for the United States in 1941. We crossed the USSR by the Siberian Express which carried German, Austrian, Czechoslovakian refugees. Ten days after our leaving Vladivostok aboard a Swedish ship, Hitler invaded the USSR. During the voyage, the ship loaded copra at Manila. Some months later, Hitler's allies invaded that island. We applied for American citizenship (first papers) on the day after Pearl Harbor.

I suppose that some poems and plays of mine, written during this period of the fight against Hitler, have moved the Un-American Activities Committee to subpoena me.

My activities, even those against Hitler, have always been purely literary activities of a strictly independent nature. As a guest of the United States, I refrained from political activities concerning this country even in a literary form. By the way, I am not a screen writer, Hollywood used only one story of mine for a picture showing the Nazi savageries in Prague. I am not aware of any influence which I could have exercised in the movie industry whether political or artistic.

Being called before the Un-American Activities Committee, however, I feel free for the first time to say a few words about American matters: looking back at my experiences as a playwright and a poet in the Europe of the last two decades, I wish to say that the great American people would lose much and risk much if they allowed anybody to restrict free competition of ideas in cultural fields, or to interfere with art which must be free in order to be art. We are living in a dangerous world. Our state of civilization is such that mankind already is capable of becoming enormously wealthy but, as a whole, is still poverty-ridden. Great wars have been suffered, greater ones are imminent, we are told. One of them might well wipe out mankind, as a whole. We might be the last generation of the specimen man on this earth.

The ideas about how to make use of the new capabilities of production have not been developed much since the days when the horse had to do what man could not do. Do you not think that, in such a predicament, every new idea should be examined carefully and freely? Art can present clear and even make nobler such ideas.

Having declined to read the statement just quoted, the Committee was under no obligation to see if the shoe fit. Instead, they fell back on the question that never failed to send an "unfriendly" to the sidelines. Was Mr. Brecht a Communist?

MR. BRECHT: Mr. Chairman, I have heard my colleagues when they considered this question not as proper, but I am a guest in this country and do not want to enter into any legal arguments, so I will answer your question as fully as well I can. I was not a member or am not a member of any Communist Party.

MR. THOMAS: Your answer is, then, that you have never been a member of the Communist Party?

MR. BRECHT: That is correct.

MR. STRIPLING: You were not a member of the Communist Party in Germany?

MR. BRECHT: No, I was not.

MR. STRIPLING: Mr. Brecht, is it true that you have written a number of very revolutionary poems, plays, and other writings?

MR. BRECHT: I have written a number of poems, and songs, and plays in the fight against Hitler, and, of course, was for the overthrow of that government.

MR. THOMAS: Mr. Stripling, we are not interested in any works that he might have written, advocating the overthrow of Germany, or the government there.

MR. STRIPLING: Yes, I understand.

But clearly, if Mr. Stripling understood, it did not hamper him from continuing a line of attack against Brecht that quoted precisely those pieces written against Hitlerism as evidence against him. Not only did Mr. Stripling quote them, but he misquoted them, and had the misfortune of being contradicted in the meaning of his translation of Brecht's works by the interpreter the Committee itself had furnished.

Brecht was expected to recall interviews twenty years past; guests who had called in his absence; and conversations over the chess board. The witness was not afraid to say that he knew the Eisler brothers, Hanns and Gerhardt, both on the Thomas Committee's griddle. He even had the courage to admit that Gerhardt Eisler had visited him. This was a tremendous revelation, and the Chair leaned forward eagerly to catch every word.

MR. BRECHT: He used to ask for his brother, who, as I told you, is an old friend of mine, and we played some games of chess, too, and we spoke about politics.

Politics! The man admitted that he talked with a known Communist about politics!

MR. STRIPLING: Politics?

MR. BRECHT: Yes.

J. Parnell Thomas craned forward, "What was that last answer?" he gasped, "I didn't get the last answer."

Stripling furnished it. "They spoke about politics."

This was a hot clue, and Sherlock Holmes could not have followed it better than Mr. Stripling did. Over hill, over dale, through more misquotations, through misunderstanding, he led the merry chase, and again, after twenty minutes, Stripling wistfully asked: "Mr. Brecht, did you ever make application to join the Communist Party?"

Mr. Brecht answered in the immortal words of J. Parnell Thomas: "No, no, no, no, no," and on his own, added a decisive "Never."

That should have satisfied even the Chairman, but it did not. He wanted to know if the Eisler brothers, Gerhardt and Hanns had ever asked him to join the Communist Party. Wearily, Mr. Brecht said: "No, no. I think they considered me just as a writer who wanted to write and do as he saw it, but not as a political figure."

The Chairman made a last try. Did *anyone* ever ask Mr. Brecht to join the Communist Party?

Mr. Brecht revealed some people might have suggested it to him. At this, the Chairman took a new lease on life.

MR. THOMAS: Who were those people who asked you to join the Communist Party?

MR. BRECHT: Oh, readers.

MR. THOMAS: Who?

MR. BRECHT: Readers of my poems or people from the audiences. You mean—there was never an official approach for me to publish—

MR. THOMAS: Some people did ask you to join the Communist Party.

MR. BRECHT: In Germany, you mean in Germany?

MR. THOMAS: No; I mean in the United States.

MR. BRECHT: No, no, no.

MR. THOMAS: He is doing all right. He is doing much better than many other witnesses you brought here.

That remark was addressed to the lawyers for the ten "unfriendlies." The sweetness and light that the Chairman now displayed, only served to point up his satifaction with a job well done, and the glorious anticipation of the surprise well-staged. Were there going to be more glamorous luminaries on the witness stand than Cooper, Taylor, and Montgomery? Chairman Thomas relaxed, and allowed Mr. Stripling to misquote one more of Mr. Brecht's poems.

MR. STRIPLING: (reading) "Forward, we've not forgotten. We have a world to gain. We shall free the world of shadow; every shop and every room; every road and every meadow. All the world will be our own." Did you write that, Mr. Brecht?

MR. BRECHT: No, I wrote a German poem, but that is very different from this. (Laughter)

The Chairman smiled. "Thank you, Mr. Brecht," he said, looking at his watch. "You are a good example to the witnesses of Mr. Kenny and Mr. Crum."

And smiling again, as he thought of the sensation he was going to create with his surprise witness, the Chairman called a recess until two o'clock that afternoon, when the crowded courtroom, and the world would discover what Mr. Thomas' private oracle had in store for them.

At two o'clock, the meeting came to order. The first witness on the stand was the handsome Louis J. Russell who was making his eleventh appearance.

So routine had his previous appearances been, that everyone fidgeted and yawned. They were impatient to hear the big news break.

For the eleventh time, Russell told who he was, what he was and that he had worked for the F.B.I. Why he no longer works there was never discussed. It seemed to the audience that Russell was only the curtain-raiser for the main event. And he droned on and on, talking about the "International Theater," the International Union of the Revolutionary Theater, and the National Convention of the Communist Party on the Cultural Commission within the United States. Frankly, no one in the courtroom was interested, except Thomas and his Committee. For they alone knew where all this was leading. They sat with calculated nonchalance, like the backers of a play, as Stripling took the lid off the "surprise," but gave only the first, tantalizing glimpse.

MR. STRIPLING: Mr. Russell, can you tell the Committee whether or not the Soviet Government has ever sent an official representative to the motion picture industry?

MR. RUSSELL: Yes.

The slumbering audience awakened. This was it! Or was it?

The Chairman, pleased with the audience's lively reaction, asked for order, and a new form of testimony was read into the record. It was never disclosed whether Russell had Elsa Maxwell or Walter Winchell as his informant, but he knew who had dinner with whom, and when. The only thing he neglected to say, was who picked up the check.

The Soviet emissary, as Mr. Russell identified him, was one Mikhial (sic) Kalatozov, who appeared in Hollywood during the Summer of 1943. Tovarisch Kalatozov was first presented in the typically Communist Party manner. He was given a cocktail party at the Mocambo, one of the plushiest cafés in Hollywood. Furthermore, Mr. Kalatozov had lived on Los Feliz Boulevard, which was dangerously close to the homes of Hollywood's best-known stars. He had even communicated to Moscow by cablegram. Typical of the messages was:

> Immediately Inform if Warner Brothers' Films
> Brought to Moscow Were Seen by You.

Suddenly it became apparent that Louis J. Russell and none other, was the long awaited Surprise Witness. The audience and the non-Hearst press had been led to expect the unveiling of an escaped member of the Politburo, or at least a woman spy —reeking of *mysterioso*. Instead what they got was li'l old Louis Russell!

There was no disguising of the fact that the audience felt badly let down. But Thomas, beaming in his seat, rolling his head around to smile knowingly at friends, indicated by his manner, however, that there was more to come.

And it came.

By dribs and drabs, and a mumbo-jumbo, hodge-podge of association, the super-sleuth jumped from Los Angeles to San Francisco to Washington, D.C.; back to Hollywood; thence to Philadelphia; to Moscow; to Berkeley, Calif.; to the Jefferson Apts., 16th and M Street, NW, Washington, D.C.; Hollywood again; to the OWI, and Robert E. Sherwood, who really had nothing to do with the case, as Mr. Russell made clear in a moment.

Then Russell picked up the daisy chain at the American Embassy in Montevideo, Uruguay, followed it to Mexico, stretched it to Paris, and snapped back to New York, listened to a speech by Molotov before the United Nations Conference at San Francisco, and somehow, gave the impression that by now, he had established a connection between the movie colony and Moscow. Indeed, he was able to throw in a few more names, a few more dates, and winding up like a pitcher, he got to The Great Revelation.

It seemed that a George Charles Eltenton, a one-time employee of the Shell Development Corp. in Emeryville, Calif., approached one Haakon Chevalier, a professor at the University of California, who Mr. Stripling suspected once was a writer in the film industry. Mr. Chevalier, in turn, approached a scientist, employed in the radiation laboratory, J. Robert Oppenheimer, the same J. Robert Oppenheimer who was in charge of the atomic bomb project at Los Alamos, New Mexico.

Mr. Chevalier asked Mr. Oppenheimer for information that Eltenton could relay to the Soviet Government. Mr. Oppenheimer was quoted saying that he considered such attempts as this, to secure information, a treasonable act, and that he, certainly, would not have anything to do with such a thing. In short, the answer was no.

This, then, was the smash ending to the publicized serial, *The Great Atomic Robbery,* produced by the Thomas Committee, starring the Surprise Witness, Louis J. Russell.

That's all?

That's all!

The audience was left hovering in space, between the floor and the ceiling of the Caucus Room.

The majestic dud lay there like a slab of uncooked veal.

And J. Parnell Thomas, to a rapidly-emptying hall spoke his valedictory:

The hearings today conclude the first phase of the Committee's investigation of Communism in the motion-picture industry. While we have heard 39 witnesses, there are many more to be heard. The Chair stated earlier in the hearing he would present the records of 79 prominent people associated with the motion-picture industry who were members of the Communist Party or who had records of Communist affiliations. We have had before us 11 of these individuals. There are 68 to go. This hearing has concerned itself principally with spotlighting Communist personnel in the industry.

I want to emphasize that the Committee is not adjourning sine die, but will resume hearings as soon as possible. The Committee hearings for the past 2 weeks have clearly shown the need for this investigation. Ten prominent figures in Hollywood whom the Committee had evidence were members of the Communist Party were brought before us and refused to deny that they were Communists. It is not necessary for the Chair to emphasize the harm which the motion-picture industry suffers from the presence within its ranks of known Communists who do not have the best interests of the United States at heart. The industry should set about immediately to clean its own house and not wait for public opinion to force it to do so.

The hearings are adjourned.

COUNTER-ATTACK

IN those last days of October 1947, the nation watched with a kind of incredulous fascination the spectacle of a gavel in the small, pink hand of an erstwhile stock-broker being used to slap shut the mouths of man after man who dared to invoke the Constitution of the United States.

The attack was not unprecedented. The elements of the Thomas-Rankin Committee pattern have been repeated many times in the political history of the United States. What was new here was the frankness, the virulence, and the inclusiveness of the attack.

Here was a "package deal" in the onslaught against civil liberties. Here, all wrapped up together, were the truculent attempt to establish censorship over the screen; the invasion of the privacy of individual belief by the drumhead trial in which men summoned to Washington because their views did not coincide with those of J. Parnell Thomas and William Randolph Hearst were exposed to severe punishment and denied opportunity to cross-examine those who had accused them; and in passing, dragging down to a new low the dignity of the nation's highest legislative body.

So the nation watched. The headlines grew larger. The radio "ringside" reports from Washington became more frenetic.

It was recognized by millions of Americans that this thing was important. Its implications struck home; the realization spread that the chips were down now. Dalton Trumbo cried out from the witness stand into the network microphones, "This is the beginning of concentration camps in America!" and a chill autumnal wind seemed to blow across the land from those October hearings in Washington.

But it was not the clammy chill of death, so much feared by some Americans of little faith. This cold wind out of Washington did not freeze with terror the American heart, as expected by Mr. Thomas and those who pull the strings which make him dance. Instead, it had a tonic effect. Its tingling shock brought healthy new blood to the surface of our national life. It revitalized concern for our democratic processes.

The counter-attack against the Thomas Committee assault on American liberty and tradition began to form in the first days of the hearings. Its momentum carried it into the new year, 1948—growing—snowballing. It included newspapers of both conservative and liberal opinion, churches, women's organizations, radio commentators, educators, the creative men and women of the motion picture industry, specially-formed committees, and millions of individual Americans.

CHAPTER 16

"We hold these hearings to be morally wrong. . . ."

ONE evening in September 1947, a group of motion picture directors, actors, and writers met at Lucey's Restaurant in Hollywood, directly opposite the RKO and Paramount studios. The meeting was arranged by William Wyler and John Huston, directors; Philip Dunne, the writer; and Alexander Knox, the screen star. It was a small meeting. But the creative achievements of every person who attended are written large in the history of the film industry. And the results of that meeting were to be written even larger in the contemporary history of our nation and the time we live in.

For here was the inception of the Committee for the First Amendment.

Behind this Committee was the clear and growing realization that the immediate objective of the Thomas Committee was to throw a road block of terror across the continuing development of the major international opinion-forming agency, the motion picture screen.

The men and women who were the prime organizers of this Committee knew film history, for they had helped to make it: First, half a century ago, had come the moving picture. Then, a couple of decades ago, the talking picture. And now, still struggling for recognition, the thinking picture—the picture with something to say.

The thinking picture had been winning its struggle for studio recognition and box office success. Its current exemplars were such hits as *Crossfire, Body and Soul, Gentlemen's Agreement, The Best Years of Our Lives*—pictures that not only moved and talked and entertained, but at the same time moved the mind to greater clarity, compassion and understanding.

These pictures talked in a language people proved at the box office they were eager to hear. These and similar pictures talked of such things as bad housing, unemployment, profiteering and high prices, Jew-baiting, Negro-baiting, fascism in America, illiteracy, inflation, poll taxes, boom-and-bust, war. They dealt with insistent realities rather than with the overworked suggestion that life in the United States is a perpetually pleasant, romantic idyll.

Naturally, the creative producers, directors, writers, and actors in Hollywood wanted to make a fair proportion of such pictures that are successful both in terms of the box office and of valid artistic maturity.

But such pictures moved to anger Representative John E. Rankin, the racist poll-taxer of Mississippi, and his committee colleague, J. Parnell Thomas. They struck terror into the heart of William Randolph Hearst, the employer of Mussolini and the supporter of Francisco Franco. The honesty and success of these pictures ruffled the delicate sensibilities of the Hearst-sponsored Motion Picture Alliance for the Preservation of American Ideals, whose members wanted to stick strictly to the one-two-three escape formula, with a little music on the side.

These people, who had been acting as the informers, men-at-arms and hand-maidens of the Thomas Committee, put the finger of subversion on such pictures as *The Best Years of Our Lives,* which swept the Academy Award field in 1947; *None But the Lonely Heart,* because it showed poverty and despair; *Margie,* for no reason that was ever plain; *Mission to Moscow* and *Song of Russia,* made as a salute to a war-time ally, and defended by the studio heads responsible for them.

Out of this conflict between screen development and retardation, maturity, and infantilism, and the use of a Congressional committee by the forces trying to keep people from seeing the kind of pictures they have proved they want to see, came the first counter-attack from Hollywood.

Almost at once it became plain that deeply underlying this attack on screen freedom, and implicit in it, was an attack on the essential idea of American liberty.

The Screen Directors' Guild issued the following statement

early in October, and it was concurred in by the Screen Writers'
Guild on October 13, 1947:

"1. Official investigations into the political beliefs held by individuals are in violation of a sacred privilege guaranteed the citizen in
this free Democracy.

"2. Such investigations are an abuse of the right of Congress to
inquire into the matters of national interest.

"3. Official attempts to restrict individual expressions of opinion are
likewise a violation of one and an abuse of the other.

"4. Any attempt on the part of an official body to set up arbitrary
standards of Americanism is in itself disloyal to both the spirit and the
letter of our Constitution.

"5. If any threat to our constitutional government is presented by
subversive elements within the country, the machinery for combating
and overcoming such is already in existence; namely, our law enforce-
ment agencies and the courts. To assume the prerogative of those
properly designated bodies amounts to charging them with incapability
of maintaining law and order, and, in the light of their splendid records, such a charge is completely unwarranted.

"6. As Americans, devoted to our country and the Constitution,
which is its spiritual shape and form, we hereby resolve to defend the
reputation of the industry in which we work against attack by the
House Committee on Un-American Activities, whose chosen weapon is
the cowardly one of inference and whose apparent aim is to silence
opposition to their extremist views, in the free medium of motion
pictures."

An earlier statement of policy adopted by the membership of
the Screen Writers' Guild warned that the immediate targets
of the Thomas Committee were the democratically administered
guilds and unions of the motion picture industry.

The Screen Writers' Guild pointed out that the ultimate
target of this committee was American democratic rights in
general, and proposed that "the various guilds, unions, and
producer organizations in Hollywood unite in opposition to the

[137]

conspiracy against the motion picture industry between a few individuals in the industry and the controlling faction of the House Committee on Un-American Activities."

The Committee for the First Amendment, subsequently formed, represented the broadest cross-section of Hollywood directors, actors, writers, publicists, and technicians, and many national leaders in the fields of literature, the theater, education, politics, and science.

Within forty-eight hours after its founding early in October 1947, the first public statement was issued:

We the Undersigned, as American Citizens who believe in constitutional democratic government, are disgusted and outraged by the continuing attempt of the House Committee on Un-American Activities to smear the Motion Picture Industry.

We hold that these hearings are morally wrong because:

Any investigation into the political beliefs of the individual is contrary to the basic principles of our democracy;

Any attempt to curb freedom of expression and to set arbitrary standards of Americanism is in itself disloyal to both the spirit and the letter of the Constitution.

The signers of that statement represented the honor roll of achievement in the film industry, in literature and in public life. They included four United States senators—Harley Kilgore of West Virginia, Claude Pepper of Florida, Elbert Thomas of Utah, and Glenn Taylor of Idaho.

As the Committee for the First Amendment grew and passed the 500-member mark, it issued the following statement of policy:

We, the Committee for the First Amendment, espouse no political party. We represent no motion picture studios. We are in no way involved in attacking or defending any individuals connected with the hearings in Washington. We are a group of five hundred independent private citizens who believe we must take action to inform the American people of the danger to their liberties. Not only the freedom of the screen but also freedom of the press, radio, and publishing are in jeopardy. Even at the risk of being called "Reds" by those who deliberately refuse to make important distinctions, our chief concern is still to protect and defend the First Amendment to the Constitution of the United States.

In Washington, the "friendly" witnesses, safe in the arms of Congressional immunity, began tattling and cackling their hearsay evidence about other men. Writers, actors, directors, and producers of the Motion Picture Alliance and even higher Hollywood echelons were doing their best to provide for Hearst and Thomas the headlines they wanted, and smirking in gratitude when the Committee condescended to patronize them with a word of thanks.

At the same time, the Hearst newspapers throughout the nation exploded a carefully timed campaign for a federal police censorship of the motion picture industry.

Emblazoned on the front pages owned by Mr. Hearst was this boldface message: "The need is for FEDERAL CENSORSHIP OF MOTION PICTURES. The Constitution PERMITS it. The law SANCTIONS it. The safety and welfare of America DEMAND it!" (Capitalization Mr. Hearst's.—Ed.)

It was quite a show—while it lasted. However, for Mr. Adolphe Menjou, Mr. Robert Taylor, Mr. Ronald Reagan, Mr. Robert Montgomery, and the lesser luminaries and satellites, it didn't last very long.

The counter-attack was gaining force. The most responsible newspapers in the nation were insistently suggesting there was something a little obscene in this vaudeville show in Washington. They pointed out that these repetitive acts, in which J. Parnell Thomas' performers used their immunity to attack the reputations and livelihoods of their industry colleagues, was not quite in accord with the American ideals to whose preservation the Motion Picture Alliance is dedicated.

The headlines began to shrink. The limelight grew colder. Daily, fewer autograph albums were thrust at the well-rehearsed stars of this strange show.

As the House Un-American Activities Committee extravaganza began to peter out from the effects of self-exposure and travesty, a new drama was emerging in Hollywood. It was destined for a tremendous national impact.

CHAPTER 17

"Will it be possible to make a broadcast like this a year from today?"

A GIGANTIC backfire of publicity was started by the Committee for the First Amendment in the third week of October 1947.

It was sparked by such creative leaders in the industry as Paul Henreid, Sterling Hayden, Evelyn Keyes, John Huston, Humphrey Bogart, Lauren Bacall, Philip Dunne, William Wyler, Gene Kelly, Danny Kaye, Marsha Hunt, Jane Wyatt, Ira Gershwin, and many, many more.

They chartered a transport plane for a flight to Washington.

They arranged for two national broadcasts over the coast-to-coast network of the American Broadcasting Company. They carried into millions of American homes the truth about what was going on in Washington, describing it as the story of "informers, spies, invasions of privacy and the other violations of rights after the manner of dictatorships and police states."

These undertakings were neither easy nor cheap. They were costly in terms of organizational effort and money. Throughout the United States the effort was forthcoming. The money was raised, with J. Parnell Thomas contributing greatly to the financial campaign each time he banged his gavel and yelled: "No, no, no, no, no!"

The Hollywood collaborationists with the Thomas Committee used every contractual trick and every personal pressure to keep the stars and directors and writers off the air and out of that Washington-bound plane.

But on October 26 and November 2, 1947, the Committee for the First Amendment was on the air with two broadcasts, directed by Norman Corwin, and including the most distinguished scientists, political leaders, writers, actors, directors, lawyers in the United states.

After the second broadcast, Frank Sinatra said: "If this (Un-American Activities) Committee gets a green light from the American people, will it be possible to make a broadcast like this a year from today?"

On October 28, the Committee for the First Amendment was en route to Washington by air, with John Huston, Humphrey Bogart, William Wyler, Paul Henreid, Danny Kaye, and many others heading to carry the counter-attack against the Thomas Committee to the American people.

This backfire proved enormously effective. Now the Thomas Committee had real competition for the headlines. On the air and in the press, in San Francisco, Chicago, New York, in every American city, town, and village as well as in Washington and Hollywood the warning reached them from such people as Thomas Mann, Thurman Arnold, Fredric March, Helen Gahagan Douglas, Charles Boyer, Senator Claude Pepper, Harlow Shapley, John Garfield, alerting them to danger.

These men and women about whose sincerity and right to speak there can be no question sounded the warning against a *coup d'état* aimed not only at the freedom of the screen but at the very heart of constitutional freedom in the United States.

The response was immediate. The tempo of newspaper and radio criticism of the Thomas Committee was at once intensified. The *New York Times,* the New York *Herald Tribune,* the *Washington Post,* the *Detroit Free Press* and hundreds of other newspapers reemphasized the dangerous implications of the Thomas Committee procedures. Radio commentators began to speak with new clarity and courage about the real meaning of this attempted Congressional invasion of the guaranteed individual right to privacy of opinion and conscience.

Before the motion picture personalities representing the Committee for the First Amendment departed from Washington they called upon the clerk of the House of Representatives and presented to him, as citizens, a petition for redress of grievances, which read:

We, the undersigned citizens of the United States residing in the State of California, do hereby respectfully petition the Honorable

Joseph W. Martin, Jr., and our Representatives in Congress, for redress of our grievances as we are privileged to do by the First Amendment to the Constitution.

As citizens of a free country, we repose our trust and faith in the first ten Amendments to the Constitution (The Bill of Rights). In our opinion, the procedures adopted by the House Committee on Un-American Activities here persistently violated the civil liberties of American citizens, to the end that today no citizen is secure from informers, spies, invasions of privacy and the other violations of rights common to dictatorships and police states.

As citizens of a great nation facing outward to the world, we believe the most powerful and persuasive argument for our way of life against all others is that provided by the free media of expression, including the press, radio and motion picture films. In our opinion the procedures adopted by the House Committee on Un-American Activities, in inquiring into the content of motion pictures which will be exhibited overseas, are damaging one of the most important instruments of expression available to the American people in presenting the case for their way of life in the entire world.

As citizens of the first and greatest democracy, we believe that every social problem can be solved by the democratic process, provided that the ballot remains secret and inviolable and provided that all the media of expression remain free of intimidation or coercion by any agency of the government. In our opinion procedures adopted by the House Committee on Un-American Activities evince a lack of faith in the democratic process and the implied belief that our way of life is too weak to resist criticism and inquiry. In so doing we believe that this Committee is making a mockery of a foreign policy which seeks to demonstrate to the world the strength and unity of our democracy.

As Members of the Committee for the First Amendment representing a large group of actors, directors, writers, and producers in the motion picture industry, we have come to Washington to attend hearings of the House Committee on Un-American Activities. We have observed and have reported our findings to those who are unable to come. They have instructed us to speak for them and to express their sense of outrage over the abuses of civil liberties which we believe to have occurred at these hearings.

In our opinion, the following abuses have occurred:

I. The investigative function of the Committee on Un-American Activities has been perverted from fair and impartial procedures to un-fair, partial and prejudiced methods.

II. The reputations and characters of individuals have been smeared and besmirched in the following manner:

a. The Committee on Un-American Activities has been guilty of a violation of the long established Anglo-Saxon-American principles of individual accountability. They have accomplished this by adopting the "mass guilt" principle, i.e. guilt by association. Not only have the subpoenaed witnesses suffered by these methods, but mass lists have been publicized that contained many names of other people. These people were included in lists which have been designated by Committee members and counsel as "subversive," "pinko," "radical," "communistic," "disloyal," "un-American," etc. These people were neither subpoenaed nor given the opportunity to defend their characters.

b. The proceedings of the Committee have come to be regarded by the American people as a criminal trial. Nevertheless, American citizens have not been given the American privilege of ordinary self-defense statements and the right to cross examine their accusers. The accused witnesses have become defendants in fact, have not been allowed the right of obtaining witnesses to testify on their behalf. Neither have they been allowed the full right of professional counsel in the defense of their characters.

c. Moreover, while theoretically the Committee is not supposed to apply punitive measures, because of its procedural abuses, it has punished individuals in a far more damaging way than the assessment of fines or personal imprisonment. They have done this by besmirching and damaging man's most precious possession, his reputation.

In view of the above stated abuses of civil rights by the House Committee on Un-American Activities, we respectfully petition the Government for a redress of grievances.

[143]

Robert Ardrey	Anne Frank	Evelyn Keyes
Humphrey Bogart	Ira Gershwin	Danny Kaye
Larry Adler	Sheridan Gibney	Arthur Kober
Lauren Bacall	Sterling Hayden	Marsha Hunt
Geraldine Brooks	Mrs. Sterling Hayden	Robert Presnell, Jr.
Jules Block	June Havoc	Henry Rogers
Richard Conte	David Hopkins	Sheppard Strudwick
Philip Dunne	Paul Henreid	Joe Sistrom
Melvin Frank	John Huston	Jane Wyatt
	Gene Kelly	

For a little while, at least, even the League of Frightened Producers took heart as they saw the results of this public action against reaction. Their spokesmen, the smiling Eric Johnston and the eminent Paul V. McNutt, found the courage to defy the Thomas Committee and to assert that the motion picture industry would not bow to the censorship of fear.

This display of managerial valor, as will later be shown, was destined to fizzle out ignominiously.

Now the committee of a handful, organized in a motion picture colony restaurant in Hollywood has grown into the national Committee of One Thousand. Dr. Harlow Shapley, the world-famed astrophysicist who heads the Harvard University Observatory, is its acting chairman. Among its active members are Dr. Frank Aydelotte, William Rose Benét, Van Wyck Brooks, Henry Seidel Canby, Norman Corwin, Olin Downes, Dr. Irwin Edman, Dr. Albert Einstein, Florence Eldridge, Mrs. Marshall Field, Dorothy Canfield Fisher, Dean Christian Gauss, Dr. Hiram Hayden, Helen Keller, Dr. Isaac M. Kolthoff, Archibald MacLeish, Fredric March, Dr. Wesley Mitchell, Dr. William Ogburn, Rexford Tugwell, and Rabbi Stephen S. Wise.

The Committee of One Thousand is working for the abolition of the House Committee on Un-American Activities, as it is at present constituted under the leadership of J. Parnell Thomas and John E. Rankin. Said the Committee of One Thousand in its first public statement:

Believing profoundly in the letter and spirit of the Bill of Rights, we are gravely disturbed by the continued attacks by men in our Government upon the freedoms guaranteed in the First Amendment to our Constitution.

We are devoted to the best in the American tradition. We believe, therefore, that the Committee on Un-American Activities threatens those freedoms that have given us for 170 years the life we cherish and respect.

They are betrayers of American ideals—those who use terror, innuendo, hearsay and smears, ignoring the common rules of evidence and all precepts of fair play.

We call upon the American people to disavow such subversions of our basic freedoms as lie in the proceedings of the Committee on Un-American Activities.

That there may be a swift termination to such assaults upon our constitutional rights, we ask the American people to join us in a concerted action towards one goal: the abolition of the Committee on Un-American Activities.

Solely to accomplish this end, we are organizing as the Committee of One Thousand. Our means: an educational program using every available medium of communication to reach the broadest section of the American people and to enlist them in this fight.

When the Washington hearings were at an end, and ten men were cited for contempt of Congress for respecting the Constitution and having faith in its guarantees, a new and immediate need arose. More money had to be raised for their defense incidental to the broader task of preserving civil and constitutional rights in the United States.

Out of urgent necessity the Freedom From Fear Committee was born. An association of Hollywood citizens, it undertook no platform of principles. It dedicated itself to the immediate matters of arranging for legal counsel, of managing speaking tours for the offense—for the vital counter-attack against the subversion of American life by the Thomas-Hearst-Gerald L. K. Smith coalition and the sinister forces it represents.

Meanwhile, other professional allies took the field, principally the Authors' League of America, Inc., comprising the

Authors', Dramatists', Radio Writers' and Screen Writers' Guilds, which issued this strong statement.

The Council of the Authors' League protests against the immoderate, uncontrolled, and radically harmful form of censorship now being exercised on the entire profession of writing by the Congressional Committee on Un-American Activities.

We do not deny the right of Congress to investigate for legislative purposes but we stand whole-heartedly opposed to the present practice of this Committee on Un-American Activities. By denying to an author the accepted democratic safeguard of witnesses in his own defense or the elementary right of cross examination, this Committee has encouraged witnesses to make unsupported public charges which blacken the author's reputation, and has thus clearly constituted a form of censorship dangerous to the rights and economic subsistence of all authors. Carried to its logical extremity this method of censorship by defamation has already affected not only some of our League members but can affect all who deal in any way with writing for public dissemination.

The motion picture industry has cravenly submitted to this censorship by blacklisting from employment a group of writers for their alleged political beliefs. These are the effects of this sort of arbitrary censorship.

The intent of censorship is to deny to the individual author, his publisher, and producer, the right to distribute and sell the product of his intelligence and his art. In the past this has commonly operated only against a work produced and issued to the public, and only to one work at a time. The author so censored has had the opportunity to oppose and refute the specific accusations in courts of law.

Here, however, we are faced with a different form of censorship. Here the man *himself* is proclaimed suspect. And the Committee has avoided, as probably fatal to its whole malign project, the necessity of impugning the author's work in detail. Indeed, the whole corpus of a man's work, past and future, is thus declared suspect. It is obvious that any who buy and use the work of that author are to be clearly warned that they may be adjudged collaborators with a citizen so arbitrarily declared to be subversive, and may thus themselves be subject to the same calumny and suspicion, open to the same grave yet unproven charge of conduct contrary to the interests of their country.

We repeat, the motion picture industry has already submitted to this warning. There has thus been established a method and a principle of censorship, fiercely unfair, basically undemocratic, and deeply un-American. We therefore earnestly and urgently protest this unwarranted and insidious censorship with all the power at our command.

The press generally kept abreast of the news events concerning the Hollywood issue in that it reported faithfully the advance of the civil and criminal cases of the ten witnesses. But it gave, as a rule, little space to the scores of resolutions of protest and calls for action which were adopted by groups on every economic and professional level throughout the country.

One of these resolutions, however, could not be ignored. It was passed by the National Institute of Arts and Letters late in February. It bore the signatures—from A to Z—from Franklin P. Adams to William Zorach, of 129 members of the National Institute. A handful of their colleagues deemed it too strong. It read:

We, the undersigned, a group of members of the National Institute of Arts and Letters, an honorary organization of American writers, artists and musicians, protest against the methods employed by the Committee on Un-American Activities of the House of Representatives in its examination of certain writers recently summoned before it.

The investigative powers of Congress are proper and important powers. They include without question the power to inquire into activities dangerous to the people and government of the United States. But like all powers exercised by a democratic government they must be exercised with a proper and decent regard for the liberties of the citizen.

It seems clear to us that the Committee on Un-American Activities of the House of Representatives has not exercised its powers in this way. On the contrary the Committee, under the chairmanship of Congressman J. Parnell Thomas of New Jersey, has employed methods which menace the fundamental rights of the American people.

Under the American Constitution and under American law it was understood from the foundation of the Republic down to the present, an accused person could defend himself in court by calling witnesses in his own behalf and by confronting and cross-examining witnesses against him; he could defend himself out of court by bringing action for libel and slander; and he was protected in preliminary investigations before the grand jury by the privacy which, under American law, surrounds such proceedings.

All these safeguards and guarantees are rejected or denied under Mr. Thomas' procedure. The accused may not call witnesses on his own behalf. He may not confront or cross-examine witnesses against him. He is not protected by privacy, since the whole proceeding is open to press, radio, motion pictures and public.

Nor, since the entire hearing and all reports of it are privileged, may he defend his reputation by suits for libel or slander. If he demands the rights of the courtroom he is told that he is not in court but under investigation. If he asks for the rights of a person under investigation he is pictured as wishing to hide the truth. If he attempts to protect his reputation against libels and slanders he is told that he has no remedy.

The result is that a man may find his reputation permanently impaired in the minds of millions of his countrymen on the basis of evidence inadmissible in a court of law without having had any opportunity at any point or by any means to confront his accusers or to defend himself. Who can foresee who next will be subjected to this disastrous procedure?

We therefore regard this as a subversion of the traditional American sense of fair play and human decency. The fact that these methods were employed in an effort to expose Communist activities in the United States, and the further fact that the Communists, if they were in a position to do so, would undoubtedly use methods as bad or worse, does not seem to justify Congressman Thomas' conduct or the conduct of his committee.

We sign this protest as members of the National Institute as well as in our capacity as private citizens because our interests as writers and artists and musicians are deeply involved. The right of any American to think as he pleases and to say what he thinks is a right of particular importance to us because upon it rests the freedom of the creative artist and, by consequence, the vitality of the creative arts.

The methods employed by the Committee on Un-American Activities result in an indirect form of censorship. This is proved by the recent action of the motion picture industry in blacklisting the writers who defied the Committee. Such censorship, even in the case of those whose political beliefs we vigorously oppose endangers the very structure of our traditional free art and free literature in the United States.

As writers, artists and musicians we submit that Congress should take immediate steps to remedy the procedure used by its investigating committees, and to guarantee to the American people that no such attack on our liberties shall reoccur.

Another 200 men and women active in the arts and unaffiliated for this purpose with any professional group, convened a Stop Censorship Rally in New York. Over the signature of Christopher La Farge, they sent this resolution and its appended Declaration of Resistance to Hollywood:

BE IT RESOLVED: That this meeting considers that all the issues involved in the present fight for freedom from censorship, freedom from blacklist, freedom from dictation—plain human freedom of expression in every branch of creative work—are bound up in the case of the Ten Hollywood writers, who are charged with contempt of Congress, and who will stand trial on that charge within the next few weeks;

That the cause of these Ten is the cause, not only of men and women in the creative professions, stage, radio, motion pictures, newspapers and literature, but of all citizens of America wishing to defend their Constitutional rights;

That these Ten are the shock troops, representing all of us in the struggle against censorship; and that one of our first purposes must be to give support to these Ten who stand in urgent need of it—their own personal savings having been exhausted in this public fight so far; and that funds be raised for the Freedom From Fear Committee which has been formed and is now at work for the specific end of meeting costs of the trials of these Ten in Washington.

In no way can we strengthen free speech more quickly and more directly than by reinforcing those who now stand in the front line of the fight.

We hold that an atmosphere of freedom is vital to our work.
The witch hunters, with their terrified band of servants acting as

self-appointed censors and critics are directing a campaign of intimidation and terror against American artists and writers.

From a rapidly repeating attack on thought and its expression, a pattern emerges uncomfortably reminiscent of the Ministry of Enlightenment of the late Dr. Paul Josef Goebbels. Some among us face prison for defying these thought control inquisitors.

We hold that denial of our freedom to create is denial of the people's right to see and hear us. It is denial of their right to think.

We accept judgment of our work only by the people.

Our heritage is freedom. We hold in contempt all who would debase this heritage.

We, the undersigned, practitioners of all the arts, affix our names to this as declaration of resistance.

There exists now a gathering of the essential forces of democracy in American life to meet this Thomas-Hearst challenge. In our history so far there have been other such challenges; they have always been met and mastered. True, timid and doubting voices are raised here and there to say that the contemporary America around us is not the old America; that it has grown a little soft and lazy, and more than a little confused through the control exerted over its sources of information by the lords of the press, the radio, and the motion picture screen.

But the impact of the Thomas Committee hearings on the nation does much to negate that theory of a fat, inert America being beguiled by radio and screen inanities while being robbed of its great birthright of liberty.

The response of so many leaders of American thought and action to the challenge posed by J. Parnell Thomas, and the response of so many Americans to their leadership, is reassurance that the old America is not dead or even seriously sick.

The issue has been dramatized: On the one side the Thomas Committee and the forces it represents; on the other side, ten men who have contributed greatly to American literature and to an honest and mature screen, and who now stake their own liberty to test and safeguard the basic liberties of the millions of Americans rallying to their support as a matter of enlightened self-interest.

The counter-attack already has achieved much. It will achieve ultimate victory with the abolition of the Thomas Committee and the reaffirmation of our basic liberties by the courts and by Congress.

RETREAT

THE prayer with which Rev. James Shera Montgomery, D.D., opened the session of the House of Representatives of the Congress of the United States on Monday, November 24, 1947, began:

"Eternal God, our Father, who despiseth not the least of Thy earthly creatures, mercifully look upon our infirmities and turn us from those evils born of prejudice, impatience and intolerance. In all our obligations to our God and our country, help us eagerly to seek the best and wisest in all things, deeply conscious that to the upright there ariseth a light in the darkness."

In view of subsequent events in the House that day, it may be charitably inferred that few members were present to hear this petition. It was high noon, and as though in answer to this prayer for light, a bright sun found the Capitol dome.

On the same day, and at about the same hour, the same effulgence glowed on another convocation in New York, attended by men who bore the biggest names in the motion picture industry. They had been peremptorily summoned—from their desks in Hollywood, their cabanas in Palm Beach, and several European capitals. The command to assemble here and on this date was issued by the absentee owners, lock-stock-and-barrel of the motion picture economy of the United States.

There were no prayers.

Yet both assemblies, the prayed over and those who did not invoke divine guidance, acted curiously alike with respect to the American tradition which they professed to love—in their fashion.

And in their fashion, by two vicious sneak punches, one aimed from Washington, one from New York, struck it down—and ran.

CHAPTER 18

"I say that no Committee of Congress, nor this whole Congress itself, has the right to ask any citizen . . . what is his politics. . . ."

A HEAP of minor legislative debris occupied the rather dilatory attention of the Members of the House of Representatives for the first quarter of an hour. But at length, the galleries began filling with visitors. The well of the House filled up rapidly. The roll was called and 358 Members answered to their names. A quorum was present. Representative government spat on its hands and prepared to go to work. *Vox populi, vox Dei.*

"The Chair recognizes the Gentleman from New Jersey."

The Gentleman from New Jersey rose. From the gallery he looked foreshortened. But he was imposing none the less. One of the best tailored men in the chamber, he was, despite his short stature, imposing.

"Mr. Speaker," J. Parnell Thomas began, "by direction of the Committee on Un-American Activities, I present a privileged report which I send to the Clerk's desk."

The Gentleman from New Jersey then sat down, better to taste the sweet poison of Hearst-Patterson-Howard acclaim.

The Clerk read: . . . "The said Albert Maltz, having appeared as a witness and having been asked questions, namely: 'Are you a member of the Screen Writers' Guild?' and 'Are you now, or have you ever been, a member of the Communist Party?' which questions were pertinent to the subject under inquiry, refused to answer such questions; and as a result of the said Albert Maltz' refusal to answer the aforesaid questions, your committee was prevented from receiving testimony and information concerning a matter committed to the said committee."

Whereupon, in proof of Maltz's "refusal" to answer, the Committee's report quoted a portion of the testimony given by the writer. Not the entire testimony, but a selected portion, including that during which Maltz, by a slip of the tongue or by psychological compulsion called Mr. Stripling, "Mr. Quisling." However, there was not a word in the report of Maltz' prepared statement.

Albert Maltz's was the pilot case of the Thomas Committee in seeking Congressional citations against ten men. Without Maltz's prepared statement in the record, it was apparent that the Committee had here their strongest case.

One legislative hour was allotted to Thomas for the prosecution of his case, and that sixty minutes was his to apportion. But first the charges had to be formalized. The Clerk read again:

"Resolved, that the Speaker of the House of Representatives certify the Report of the Committee on Un-American Activities as to the refusal of Albert Maltz . . . under seal of the House of Representatives, to the United States Attorney for the District of Columbia, to the end that the said Albert Maltz may be proceeded against in the manner and form provided by law."

Which of course means that if the Congressmen assembled voted certification of the Un-American Activities Committee's report, the judicial machinery of the government was to be thrown into gear, to the end that Maltz should be convicted of contempt of the Congress and be given the maximum penalty provided: a year's imprisonment and a fine of $1,000.

J. Parnell Thomas yielded himself ten minutes of the allotted hour and used it all, and a few more, in a paen of praise for his committee and how the ship of state could barely make steerageway without its constant watch and ward. They had been notably cautious with regard to the motion pictures in which, he said:

"Communists would bend every effort to infiltrate and obtain influence in such a powerful and important medium of propaganda and education. . . ."

His talk throughout was studded with such clichés and catchphrases as "fellow travelers," "dupes," "paid apologists" and

[155]

the entire lexicon worn thin by overuse in the most blatant section of America's press. Substantially half of his remarks were devoted to a defense of the Committee and its behavior.

There has been an extensive campaign launched in the United States to vilify this committee and to confuse the American people into believing that in asking these witnesses to state whether or not they were members of the Communist Party we were invading their Constitutional rights.

Mr. Speaker, I want to say with all the sincerity that is within my heart, that one of the great mistakes that we in the United States can make is to put the Communist Party in the category of being a political party.

It mattered not to Chairman Thomas that he was fanning the air. He was, in other words, demanding an indictment of the ten men on the grounds that they neither endorsed nor opposed his opinion as to the character of the Communist Party.

He came to the climax of his peroration:

Now, Mr. Speaker, as I have stated, the issue is simple here. These witnesses refused to answer the most pertinent question that we could ask. They have with utter contempt and impunity defied a committee of this House. . . . I ask therefore that you sustain the unanimous action of the Committee on Un-American Activities in citing these individuals for contempt.

He ended with the warning that smacked of Karl H. von Weigand's purplest alarms that the world was locked in a death struggle. Red totalitarianism was at our collective windpipes. Save the American home! Beat the hammer and sickle into a juke-box! Strike now! Send these ten screen writers on their way to the federal Bastille!

"Mr. Speaker, I yield ten minutes to the Gentleman from Illinois."

This was Rep. Richard B. Vail, of Illinois who sat at Chairman Thomas' left throughout the hearings. After 5,000 words, some well-chosen, some ill, "fully endorsed," then proceeded to supplement the remarks of the Gentleman from New Jersey. He gave the "friendly" witnesses their accolade, saying that they had the "cooperative disposition" and were "sympathetic to the aims of the Committee."

But the others! Those "unfriendly" ten! They were no better than the lawyers who represented them, Vail complained. These lawyers, he said, "incidentally have themselves long been associated with efforts to defend the Communist Party or its members."

Representative Vail quoted former Attorney General Biddle's low opinion of the Communist Party which he uttered in the case against Harry Bridges, the West Coast C.I.O. leader. However, Vail did not mention that Bridges, whom Biddle sought to deport on those grounds was enjoying full American citizenship and a cocktail a block away at that moment.

At length, to clinch the charge against the Communist Party, Vail quoted, as though it were the Fifth Book of Moses—the House Un-American Activities Committee itself, which, he said, "as far back as January 3, 1940" characterized the Communist Party as a "foreign conspiracy masked as a political party."

This ingenuousness was in no way surprising to any who remembered that the Un-American Activities Committee was nine years old—a sage among Congressional committees—and that its "characterizations" are believed by now to have the force of law in some circles.

Vail possessed an additional morsel of proof—right out of the Communists' own mouths. Quoting from a pamphlet by one S. Tchernomordik, a stranger even to the scholar, Menjou, he read: *"As a result of many years of experience during the Czarist regime, the Bolsheviks came to the conclusion that the best policy was to refuse to answer any questions whatever."*

I ask therefore on behalf of the Committee on Un-American Activities, a unanimous vote to cite the witness, Albert Maltz, for contempt of Congress.

J. Parnell Thomas then graciously yielded ten minutes to Representative Eberharter of Pennsylvania. A few minutes later, he wished he hadn't.

MR. EBERHARTER: . . . Should a committee of this House expect the support of Members of this body when it flies in the face of constitutional guarantees which every American has always considered sacred. Recently the American delegate to the conference of the United Nations, the Honorable Warren Austin, solemnly warned the world against putting "shackles on the mind of man and a gag in his mouth." Should we, in deliberative session, place in fear of punishment a few American citizens who have, either misguidedly or courageously, resisted the imposition of shackles and gags.

The decision which we as Members face may be a painful one, but, as I see it, the course of honor and duty is clear. The alternatives are inescapable. Either we sustain the action, punitive in nature, of one of our committees, or we sustain the principles of our founding fathers who, in the words of the United States Supreme Court, "recognized the occasional tyrannies of governing majorities and amended the Constitution so that free speech and assembly should be guaranteed."

We can support the recommendations of the Committee on Un-American Activities for citations for contempt of Congress, or we can support free speech. We cannot have both. We must have one or the other.

It was plain that Eberharter had detected the specter of federal censorship through the thin scrim of the Thomas Committee's ragging of witnesses. Censorship was outside of the Committee's province.

"Americans know that they alone can safely censor American movies," Eberharter continued. He told the House that time and again the names of the "subversive" films with which any of the witnesses were associated were requested, and that the Committee was silent.

MR. EBERHARTER: I cannot escape the conclusion that there is some justification for the charge shared by millions of Americans, that the purpose of the Committee was not to destroy an existent subversive threat in Hollywood, but to intimidate and control the movie industry; to secure the production of movies whose Americanism content would be certified by the Members of the Committee on Un-American Activities.

If Americanism means anything, it means that no group of persons,

[158]

however exalted, can dictate what is, or is not, Americanism. In the language of our Supreme Court:

If there is any fixed star in our constitutional constellation, it is that no official, high or petty, can prescribe what shall be orthodox in politics, nationalism, religion, or other matters of opinion, or force citizens to confess by word or act their faith therein.

CHAPTER 19

"It was precisely the kind of excesses we deliber-
ate upon today that the President's Committee
on Civil Rights had in mind when it warned
against the near hysteria over Communism
which is wreaking havoc in the field of constitu-
tional safeguards."

A MONTH earlier, during the hearings, an alert spectator upon hearing the Chief Investigator say to a witness that he was charged with being a Communist (or words to that effect) said that this would some day become a prime issue.

And it did. Earlier than even was anticipated, Representative Eberharter let that cat out of the bag and laid it right in the lap of J. Parnell Thomas.

Said Eberharter,

Since the Committee was unable to show that any specific movie was Communist inspired or dictated, what could it want with the 19 witnesses? The answer is clear. In the words of the Committee's counsel (not a lawyer), the witnesses were being charged with Communism and the Committee was conducting a trial on these charges. Today we are acting in the role of a grand jury. We are being asked, in effect, to sign a true bill.

I question whether any committee of this House is empowered or can be empowered constitutionally, to try any person, on any charge, other than those involved in the constitutional provisions governing impeachment.

MR. THOMAS: The Chief Investigator never made any such statement that these witnesses were on trial.

MR. EBERHARTER: The Chief Investigator who was questioning the witnesses said: "You are being charged with being a Communist."

Thomas instantly declared that, "other witnesses charged them as being Communists . . . the word trial was never used. . . . We have no right to try anyone."

MR. EBERHARTER: I am glad to hear the gentleman say he has no right to try anybody, but your chief counsel did say: "You are charged with being a Communist." And that is what I based my statement on. . . . What are the facts? These witnesses were placed on trial and denied the right of counsel. They were confronted by witnesses who were permitted to smear them with innuendo, suspicion, prejudice, and hearsay three or four times removed, and were not granted the right to cross-examine. Charges made against them carried full legal immunity to those making them; they were given national publicity. Yet the persons charged were not permitted to testify in rebuttal when they wanted to do so. . . .

The Committee should have followed hallowed rules of evidence, Eberharter pointed out.

It should have subscribed to the doctrine of probable cause. It should have excluded rumor, gossip and mean prejudice. . . . And grave as were the evils of this so-called trial, they were immeasurably aggravated because the charges trespassed on the realm of freedom of speech and freedom of conscience.

Eberharter did not spare the lash as he asked his fellow-law makers to take a glance backward at the Un-American Activities Committee's record. They would there discover, he continued, that the Committee, from its very inception, nine years earlier, had shown "a congenital inability to recognize where the freedoms protected by the first amendment begin." Moreover, it "has branded as Un-American everything it dislikes, vilified those who have criticized it and stigmatized those who have committed the supreme crime of defying it."

"The Committee," Eberharter declared, "loosed upon its critics its full arsenal of invective and intimidation," and concluded:

If we are to avoid hysteria, let us get back to the fundamental verities. . . . I say Americans must not be silenced. They will not be

[161]

silenced or intimidated. I say that the First Amendment has placed an invincible shield around all Americans—the ten witnesses now faced with contempt citations, no less than any other Americans—that protects them from the kind of intrusion practiced in the so-called Hollywood hearings.

If we remain true to the immortal words of Thomas Jefferson, "I have sworn upon the altar of the living God eternal hostility against every form of tyranny over the mind of man," we must vote down the recommendations of the Committee on Un-American Activities.

Representative Sadowski of Michigan was given one minute, during which he gave some data to J. Parnell Thomas on the status of a citizen of Michigan with respect to political freedom.

The right of citizenship in my State, the right of ballot, the right of free ballot, of a secret ballot, will be preserved, and no congressional committee has a right to ask a man from Michigan, "What is your politics?"

I expect every member from Michigan will vote as I will against this indictment. . . .

There is another and a greater law than the laws of Michigan or of the Congress, and that is the law that Thou shalt not bear false witness against thy neighbor.

At which point the time of Rep. Sadowski expired and his Michigan colleague, Clare E. Hoffman, rose to defend the Committee as he has done for years—and the Committee in turn has defended him in the great tradition of Congressional logrolling.

A Californian, Rep. Chet Holifield was allotted four minutes. "I shall vote against these contempt citations today as a matter of principle and conscience," he said at the outset of his remarks. "A wave of fear, suspicion, and hysteria sweeps our nation today. Fear begets fear, suspicions begets suspicion and hysteria begets mob action and un-American denial of civil liberties."

He related to the House a recent incident of the kind of mob action which hysteria begot, in a suburb of Los Angeles. A legal and peaceful meeting of a Democratic club had been called in the home of a respectable, retired business man. Just as it was called to order, a mob of men, several armed, all wearing caps of a local American Legion post, burst in. They terrorized the assembled citizens and virtually read them the riot act, ordering them to disperse.

The commander of the Legion post involved at first denied that he knew anything about the incident, but later admitted that he was one of the leaders of the raiding party. This example of vigilantism earned for the participants varying fines and jail terms.

MR. HOLIFIELD: What caused this encroachment of the civil liberties of law-abiding citizens?

Are we on the verge of storm trooper incidents throughout America?

It was a Democratic Club in Montrose, Calif., November 14, 10 days ago—it may be a Catholic group, or a Jewish group, or a Republican group, or a Negro group, or a labor group next time.

Holifield was unkind enough as to remind the Un-American Activities Committee of the solitary piece of legislation which it succeeded in getting passed in Congress in the nine years of its existence. This, he recalled was an amendment to a deficiency bill which prohibited payment of salaries to three federal officials on the ground that the Committee, under the chairmanship of Martin Dies, declared the three men to be Communists.

The vote in the House in favor of their bill was 318 in favor and 62 against. The men were promptly chopped off the federal payroll and they sued in the federal courts. When their case reached the Supreme Court the legislative act was condemned as a bill of attainder in one of the most stinging opinions of recent times.

"I refuse to be sidetracked by the hysterical red-baiting, witch-hunting wave which sweeps our country after every great war," said the Californian, continuing:

The Alien and Sedition Laws were passed after the Revolutionary War and later repealed during Thomas Jefferson's administration. The Mitchell Palmer raids occurred after World War I. Seventy-six pieces of loyalty legislation were introduced during this hysterical period. None of them became law. So again we see the wave, the same wave of hysteria sweeping over America.

Are we going to present the ridiculous picture of 140,000,000 people cowering in fear of the threat of Communism?

Have we so little faith in the principles of Democracy?

Fear and suspicion is being fomented and directed against every person or group whose philosophy seems to be to the left of the accuser. Where is this to end?

If we are to sit in judgment as to the loyalty of every man or group whose opinions we oppose, who will be next?

The oratory see-sawed between opposition to the citations and approval of them. Rep. Peterson of Florida viewed the matter legalistically and came to a rather unique conclusion as to the standing at law of the ten "unfriendly" witnesses. His opinion was that the laws of the land respecting a citizen's right not to answer applied only in criminal cases. The ten witnesses not being criminals, Peterson maintained, they were bound to answer. Simple.

Rep. Johnson of California assured all that the men would eventually have the matter in the courts, so why not just vote them in contempt and let the judiciary have a crack at it.

The sands were running low in the hour-glass of the Congressional petitioners. J. Parnell Thomas yielded the balance of the time to Committeeman John McDowell, the partner of his right hand during the hearings.

Representative McDowell fell verbally upon Albert Maltz as though there had been a blood-feud between the Maltzes and McDowells for many generations.

The Congressman mentioned Thomas Jefferson as approving the tactics used by Congressional committees, but failed to quote him. He presented a harrowing picture of Europe in cringing flight before the Red specter or already in its chains.

And as for Albert Maltz, well. . . .

. . . he ducked and squirmed, screamed and equivocated, and hurled accusations and asked himself imaginary questions until he was forced from the stand.

. . . a card-carrying Communist—a dues-paying member.

Look here—here are 15 closely written pages connecting him 58 different times and occasions with known Communist activities in the United States. I ask, Mr. Speaker, unanimous consent to place this list of his activities in the RECORD at this point.

But McDowell did not stop at that point to formally receive that consent, hence the Congressional Record of that day, yields not a word of the 58-point bill of subversive particulars against the man under discussion. The Gentleman from Pennsylvania bucketed along:

There you have it. There it is. Maltz screamed and he yelled and he finally was forced from the witness stand. . . .

The citation of Albert Maltz was called here first because this man was the most arrogant, the most contemptible, the most bitter of all of these people who do not believe in their own country.

McDowell, among the committeemen also revealed himself as a bit of a literary critic in his discussion of several articles which the man he was flaying had written for—well—it must out some time—the *New Masses*. These articles were frankly controversial—so controversial that Maltz became the center of a left literary whirlpool and had the honesty to correct himself.

McDowell called this "an act of degradation . . . . that shamed him in front of every honest writer in the world."

Westbrook Pegler and George Sokolsky are two of the "honest writers" who, from time to time, still stroke their forefingers at Maltz.

MR. McDOWELL: Here you are. . . . This Maltz addressed Robert Stripling as Mr. Quisling, a world-wide synonym for traitor.

And there McDowell's voice almost broke. A note of sadness came into it as he said, "Sometimes, Mr. Speaker, one wonders if public service and love of country, with all of its great magnitude, is sufficient pull to retain a membership or employment on this difficult Congressional assignment."

Then, having called O. John Rogge, former special assistant to the Attorney General of the United States "an American Vishinsky," Mr. McDowell sat down.

[165]

Mr. Thomas: Mr. Speaker, I move the previous question.

Mr. Marcantonio: Mr. Speaker, I demand the yeas and nays.

The yeas and nays were ordered and the question taken: That Albert Maltz, writer, union affiliation and politics so far undeclared, shall be turned over to the federal authorities and forthwith prosecuted for contempt of the Congress.

The yeas numbered 346. The nays, 17—Bakewell, Blatnik, Bloom, Carroll, Celler, Douglas, Eberharter, Havenner, Holifield, Huber, Karsten (Mo.), Klein, Marcantonio, Morgan, Pfeifer, Powell, Sadowski.

In the language of the Congressional Record; "So the resolution was agreed to."

CHAPTER 20

". . . you cannot by implication—by saying,
'You did not deny it' convict the man of some-
thing you are charging against him."

IF, as Congressman McDowell said, Maltz was hauled up first
because he was "the most arrogant, contemptible and bitter of
all," Dalton Trumbo stood next in the low estimate of the
House Un-American Activities Committee.

Representative Karl E. Mundt of South Dakota, a member of
the Committee, but who attended none of its sessions pertaining
to the Hollywood case, teed off. He had been busy elsewhere
during the hearings, but he said he listened to the radio and
read the newspapers. By blithely assuring the Congressmen that
"the American public, by and large" gave approval to the work
of the Un-American Activities Committee, he had evidently not
read such newspapers as the *New York Times,* the Washington
Post and the New York *Herald Tribune.* He congratulated himself and the other 345 Congressmen who voted for the Maltz
citation. As for the 17 who didn't. . . .

. . . you find yourselves left alone, because in Hollywood their (the
witnesses') employers today are stating publicly that they want no more
to do with them until they can make up their minds whether they are
proud to be Americans. . . .

Congressman Mundt, during his peroration disclosed a fact
hitherto unknown, and certainly unpublicized: that he had
discussed the situation with "some of the leading members of
the motion picture industry itself."

MR. MUNDT: Then, to go on, I want to congratulate the Fox Moving
Picture Co., the Twentieth Century-Fox, I believe it is called, which
passed a resolution the other day and I read it to you:

[167]

Resolved. *That the officers of this corporation be, and they hereby are directed, to the extent that the same is lawful, to dispense with the services of any employee who is an acknowledged Communist or of any employee who refuses to answer a question with respect thereto by any Committee of the Congress of the United States and is cited for contempt by reason thereof.*

Mundt was definitely in a congratulatory mood. He felicitated 20th Century-Fox once more and sang out the news that the rest of the film companies are taking similar steps to "eliminate from the payroll people who make a profession of being in being *(sic)* in contempt. . . . I think that is a fine, commendable attitude."

But blacklisting these writers and directors (who Mundt said had been "accused by their employers, by their fellows, by their associates, by the people working with them") was not enough.

MR. MUNDT: The Committee on the Judiciary has a bill which was introduced by a member of our Committee early in this session which would increase the penalty for contempt of Congress from $1,000 to $5,000 and from one year to five years.

News of this bill was furnished by Rep. Graham, a member of the Committee on the Judiciary. He disclosed that 14 members of the Committee, a majority, were ready to sign a petition and go before the Committee on Rules to ask that it not be reported out. They didn't like it.

MR. MUNDT: I hope those members will have a change of heart. I understand that it is just a little quibble among lawyers about some technicality, and I think that can be ironed out, and then we laymen will have a chance to do something constructive in the matter of increasing the penalty for being in contempt of Congress.

J. Parnell Thomas gained the floor and declared that he had done everything possible to get that $5,000 fine - five-year imprisonment bill reported out.

MR. MUNDT: I am sure that if the fine members of the Committee on the Judiciary would get together and iron out their legal difficulties and propose a bill that we could enact, it would be a great public service.

THE SPEAKER: The time of the gentleman has expired.

Representative Javits of New York, to whom the floor was next granted, appeared to make considerably more sense than his Dakota colleague. He declared that the question of whether or not the ten Hollywood men were guilty of contempt is strictly a legal one. He had read the record of the hearings from cover to cover, he said.

The Committee has permitted witnesses testifying before it to charge other people on their mere assertion and without tangible proof with being Communists. Thereupon, these other people were called up and told, "There are charges against you. Do you deny them?"

When it comes to the matter of trying an individual's character, we just don't operate that way in the United States.

Javits then proceeded to quote as an example of the technique he abhorred, the examination of Alvah Bessie. And before yielding the floor, announced that he was introducing that day two resolutions; First, that the Committee on Un-American Activities as such, should be dissolved.

"It is not a committee of the House dealing with legislative matters," he said, "and should, therefore, not be one of the standing committees of the House."

Second, that a committe of the House and of the Senate with seven members from each should be appointed "to investigate all such situations which now are within the jurisdiction of the Committee on Un-American Activities."

"Such a joint committee should have rules and regulations to protect the character of individuals appearing before it. . . ."

Representative Celler of New York was awarded four minutes and it was conceded by the press and lay spectators that he made them count against the Thomas Committee. He was opposed to the use of "even a little totalitarianism to preserve our Democracy."

[169]

I deprecate, for example, the use of would-be experts like Rupert Hughes who said he could tell a Communist by his olfactory sense; he said he could smell them.

I deprecate the use of Mrs. Rogers as an expert, who had the temerity to say and to brand a film communistic if it portrayed despair and hopelessness. Shades of Edgar Allan Poe, and his despair and hopelessness.

Adolphe Menjou was permitted . . . without remonstrance to cloak thousands of innocent Americans with Communism by the astounding statement that anyone who witnesses Paul Robeson and applauds is a Communist. That is a new low in witch-hunting.

The fiery Vito Marcantonio had evidently taken the trouble to digest the prepared legal claims of the witnesses' lawyers.

MR. MARCANTONIO: Since you cannot legislate in any manner that will abridge the freedom of speech or freedom of the press, you cannot investigate this field. That is exactly what the situation is here. You are investigating in a field over which you cannot legislate; consequently the activity of the committee is in violation of the Constitution."

Certainly something further left was expected from Marcantonio. He didn't disappoint anybody.

. . . It seems that the Committee and the Congress during the last few years have taken the position that democracy is synonymous with the rule of monopoly capital; that democracy is synonymous with everything for which monopoly capital stands; that anyone who protests against the rule of monopoly capital, anyone who objects to what is transpiring under that rule; anyone who seeks social and economic change is subversive. Thus, you have been attempting to make Americans conform with the pattern of the big trusts. America will never survive if we place America in that strait-jacket.

THE SPEAKER: The time of the Gentleman from New York has expired.

J. Parnell Thomas generously yielded Marcantonio an additional minute for:

Place America in that strait-jacket and we will have the America of the standpatters. We will have the America of the Bourbons and of the Tories . . . (who) at least did not use this kind of technique to destroy the opposition. The technique of red-baiting, using the Communist bogey for the purpose of imposing fascism.

It is the weapon employed to protect the few who benefit from the program of war and depression. It is a repetition of history. It was done this way in Italy. And if I have to be alone again in this Congress I will cast my vote against it ever happening in the United States of America.

"The Hollywood hearings were a tragic farce."

Those were among the first words of Rep. Helen Gahagan Douglas, former actress and wife of Melvyn Douglas, the film star, when she addressed the House in her turn.

"While I realize," she continued, "that the procedure essential to a courtroom cannot prevail in a Congressional hearing, nevertheless Congress should provide certain safeguards to protect the witnesses appearing before committees."

She too had prepared a bill which would outline such safeguards to witnesses before Congressional groups, and hoped that her colleagues would take the time to study it.

I don't know whether or not there were any Communists among those subpoenaed. But whether people are Communists, Republican, or Democrat, they are entitled to decent and orderly treatment in accordance with American principles.

In that paragraph of her address, Mrs. Douglas stripped away the gauze of oratory and exposed the bone of contention between the liberal Congressional group and their rivals. Thomas had consistently maintained, and was to maintain again before the day was over, that constitutional rights did not apply to those whom his committee had accused of being Communists.

Mrs. Douglas: Even if the hearings had been conducted with the utmost propriety and the most careful regard for the rights of the individual, it is still a very dubious exercise of Congressional power when the Committee on Un-American Activities seeks to tell the motion picture producers what kind of pictures they should make.

[171]

The Committee, had Mrs. Douglas known it, had not only "sought to tell the producers what kind of pictures they should make," but had succeeded. In Hollywood there was a great shelving of scripts. Some of these had been written by the ten witnesses under discussion and others were scheduled for direction by other of these witnesses.

MRS. DOUGLAS: When I took my oath of office, I swore to uphold the Constitution and the Bill of Rights. Any infringement upon freedom of speech is a violation of the first amendment.

I consider it my clear duty to oppose the Committee on Un-American Activities.

Taking a page from a historic Supreme Court opinion, the gentlewoman from California said, "The argument that the hour demands extreme measures is not valid."

Before she concluded, Mrs. Douglas read to the Congressmen a resolution unanimously adopted by the House of Bishops of the Protestant Episcopal Church on November 4, 1947:

Resolved. That as bishops in the church of God we call upon the people of our church to be on their guard lest an hysterical fear of Communism shall lead us to fight that danger with weapons destructive of the treasure we seek to guard. The surest way to fight Communism is to work unceasingly at home and abroad for a society in which justice and the dignity of free men are in truth guaranteed to men of every race and condition. An inquisitorial investigation of men's personal beliefs is a threat to freedom of conscience. The casting of public suspicion on fellow-citizens under the protection of congressional immunity can readily become an offense against God's commandment, Thou shalt not bear false witness against thy neighbor. We have no defense for those, who, while sharing the privileges of our imperfectly democratic society, seek to undermine its fabric. But we hold it to be the duty of every Christian citizen to guard for others the freedom of conscience we treasure for ourselves.

MRS. DOUGLAS: Thus sayeth the bishops. And thus sayeth all of us who take our Americanism from Thomas Jefferson, Abraham Lincoln and Franklin D. Roosevelt.

CHAPTER 21

*"Mr. Speaker, I yield 7 minutes to the Gentle-
man from Mississippi, Mr. Rankin."*

THE House Un-American Activities Committee, petitioning
here mightily for the imprisonment of ten men was not always
the type of investigatory body it is today. Representative Klein,
of New York, reminded the Members that during the period of
the chairmanship of Rep. McCormack, of Massachusetts, it
adopted rules of procedure characterized "by extreme fairness
and care in preventing injustice to individuals."

It was recalled also, that during that pre-Dies period, the
Committee concerned itself mainly with investigating Nazi and
fascist organization and individuals.

Rep. Klein, too, had a bill in preparation which would amend
the rules under which the Committee operates and restore some
of the basic fairness to which witnesses are entitled:

MR. KLEIN: No man's loyalty to this country may be challenged on
the basis of his advocacy of progressive ideas, nor of his color, his
national derivation, his name or his creed, or his political beliefs.

As the New York Congressman uttered that sentence, there
was seated near him a man whose hackles must have risen. He
was Representative John E. Rankin, of Mississippi. He would
be heard from, not much later, on the very subject of the
national derivation and names of certain respectable American
citizens.

Rep. Carroll of Colorado did not like the way the Un-American Activities Committee had done things and proposed to vote
against the contempt citations despite his expressed fear that
he was on the losing side.

But I will not stand silent, or vote expediently when I believe the
basic principles of the Constitution are being placed in jeopardy. I

believe the Supreme Court will not sustain the action of Congress on this issue. . . . If the Committee is the only bulwark against communism, this Nation is, indeed, in a tragic state. . . .

The Supreme Court has ruled that we must distinguish between what one thinks and what one does. If dangerous thinking is translated into action, we have many laws which can be invoked against the offender.

Holifield, the Californian, in resuming the floor later, ventured upon some fiscal details of the Committee's operations. He cited that it had been in existence nine years and had used up $771,434.51 of the taxpayers' money. And for this

. . . the record of legislation recommended by this Committee for passage by the House: Exactly zero.

For nine years this Committee has paraded on the national scene. Its files, according to its own admission, contain a blacklist of over a million people whom they claim are either "disloyal," "subversive," "radical," "Communist" or "Un-American."

Mr. Thomas: Will the Gentleman yield?

Mr. Holifield: I yield.

Mr. Thomas: In the first place the Committee up to this year had no right to report legislation. In the second place, the Gentleman mentioned cost.

Mr. Holifield: The Gentleman is taking my time.

Mr. Thomas: I will give the Gentleman a little more time.

Thomas then expatiated on the $25,000,000 which President Truman allocated to "cleaning Communists out of the Government." And out of the portion already spent, the executive broom swept out only seven persons.

Mr. Thomas: Just compare that with the people who have gone to jail over a period of years as the result of the Committee's exposure.

Mr. Holifield: I thank the Gentleman for the contribution. I wish to ask the Gentleman in all fairness to give me the time he promised me.

Mr. Thomas: I yield the Gentleman one additional minute.

Mr. Holifield: I thank the Gentleman.

[174]

When this ponderous Congressional courtesy ended, the House, the press and the visiting public craned forward to hear a legislator who never fails to make headlines—John E. Rankin, of Mississippi, the venerable and ranking Democratic member of the House Committee on Un-American Activities.

It is Rankin, more than any other Member of Congress, whom the Committee may thank for the new lease of life it was granted by the 80th Congress. Rankin, a master parliamentarian, did it by legislative prestidigitation.

It was, in other words, palmed off, on the first day that the 80th Congress went into session.

During the October hearings Rankin had not been present at any of the sessions. He had been in Mississippi campaigning for the Senate seat to which Theodore Bilbo had been elected, but to which he never ascended. Rankin lost, decisively and ignominiously. The campaign had taught him nothing.

Rankin wound up, cut loose and made his headline:

MR. RANKIN: It has been amazing to hear these Members rise on the floor of the House to give aid and comfort to those enemies, those traitors within our gates, for every Communist in America is a traitor to the Government of the United States and is dedicated to its overthrow.

MR. MARCANTONIO: Mr. Speaker, I ask that the words of the Member be taken down.

THE SPEAKER: The Gentleman from New York demands that the words of the Gentleman from Mississippi be taken down.

MR. MARCANTONIO: That the words "that the Members gave aid and comfort to traitors" be taken down.

THE SPEAKER: The Gentleman will proceed in order.

MR. RANKIN: Now, Mr. Speaker, they attack the action of the Committee on Un-American Activities. My only objection to what the Committee did was that they should have done it quietly. The motion-picture people wanted to make a picture of it. Probably if I had been there they would not have been so keen about making pictures.

They were not only poisoning the minds of your children with their subtle Communist propaganda; but they were making pictures to be shown abroad belittling and discrediting the American people.

[175]

You have not seen a picture show in years concerning the South that did not attempt to smear and discredit the white people of the Southern States.

You would be surprised if I were to give you the name of a man, one of the great moving picture men of this country, if you please, who said he could take those pictures and show you the Communist line in a majority of them. Those men asked us to bring those witnesses here and investigate them.

MRS. DOUGLAS: Mr. Speaker, will the Gentleman yield?

MR. RANKIN: For what?

MRS. DOUGLAS: For a question.

MR. RANKIN: For a question only.

MRS. DOUGLAS: What I cannot understand . . .

MR. RANKIN: No; I do not yield for any of your understanding. I yielded for a question.

MRS. DOUGLAS: Why did not the Committee name the pictures that had this propaganda?

MR. RANKIN: Simply because the grand jury does not always give out its information in advance. Besides these Communists were using the moving-picture industry to spread their poisonous propaganda throughout the world.

I do not yield further.

Here is a petition that was sent to Congress, condemning the Committee.

MRS. DOUGLAS: Why did they not wish to see the pictures?

THE SPEAKER: The Gentleman from Mississippi declines to yield further.

MR. RANKIN: . . . They sent this petition to Congress, and I want to read you some of these names.

One of the names is June Havoc.

We found out from the motion picture almanac that her real name is June Hovick.

Another one was Danny Kaye, and we found out that his real name was David Daniel Kamirsky.

Another one here is John Beal, whose real name is J. Alexander Bliedung.

Another is Cy Bartlett whose real name is Sacha Baraniev.

Another one is Eddie Cantor, whose real name is Edward Iskowitz.

There is one who calls himself Edward Robinson. His real name is Emanuel Goldenberg.

There is another one here who calls himself Melvyn Douglas, whose real name is Melvyn Hesselberg.

There are others too numerous to mention. They are attacking the Committee for doing its duty in trying to protect this country and save the American people from the horrible fate the Communists have meted out to the unfortunate Christian people of Europe.

THE SPEAKER: The time of the Gentleman from Mississippi has expired.

In rapid order, the drum fire of citations continued. To be prosecuted for contempt of Congress—Adrian Scott, Samuel Ornitz, John Howard Lawson, Edward Dmytryk, Lester Cole, Herbert Biberman, Alvah Bessie, Ring Lardner, Jr.

Such were the proceedings on the afternoon of November 24, 1947 in the House of Representatives. It may be asked how closely the men and women who represent the people in Congress, represented the feelings of the average citizen.

The Gallup Poll culled the following figures at about the same time, publishing them on November 29, that is, five days later.

In the first place it was found that 8 out of every 10 people had heard or read about the investigation. This puts it ahead of UN or the Marshall Plan as far as the white light of publicity thrown upon it.

Those who knew something of the investigation were asked:

What is your opinion of the investigation—do you approve or disapprove of the way it was handled?

Approve	37%
Disapprove	36%
No opinion	27%

Thus while the public was about split on approval and disapproval, their so-called representatives in Congress plumped 346 to 17 in favor of the Committee.

The Gallup Poll asked another question:

Do you think the Hollywood writers who refused to say whether they were members of the Communist Party should be punished or not?

Should be	47%
Should not	39%
No opinion	14%

Here again the people were rather closely divided on this issue and again it may be said that they were not "represented" in Congress.

A breakdown of these figures prepared by the Gallup Poll gives us an even greater disparity if we take the viewpoint that Congress represents the enlightened opinion of the people.

College graduates voted 54% to 34% that the writers should not be punished.

High school graduates voted 43% to 44% that they should not be punished.

Grammar school graduates voted just about the opposite of college graduates: 53% to 31% in favor of punishment.

Congressional vote which was about 80% for punishment and about 8% against, with 12% not voting (taking into consideration some 68 members who paired off), does not really "represent" any group in our country, neither by education nor by occupation. For the Gallup Poll broke its figures down into still another category and found:

Professional and business people were 47% to 41% in favor of no punishments.

White collar workers were 51% to 41% against punishment.

Even farmers, the group voting highest in favor of punishment, did not come near the Congressional 80 to 8. Farmers voted only 62% to 23% in favor of punishment.

Certainly somebody is out of step here. Either the citizens of this country or the men they have sent to Congress to represent them.

CHAPTER 22

"We will forthwith discharge or suspend without compensation . . . any of the ten until such time as he is acquitted, or has purged himself of contempt, and declared under oath that he is not a Communist."

IN its moment of victory, in a battle for a free screen, in which writers were their natural allies, the motion picture companies suddenly, and for the moment unaccountably, submitted to defeat.

It was one of the most dizzying retreats in the history of American industrial enterprise. The film industry became the first mass-employer to adopt the blacklist as a recognized policy to be used against persons whose political beliefs may not coincide with the prevailing orthodoxies. Other industries may have their blacklists too, in pale ink, oral directives, or in code on executives' desks, but the motion picture business is the first to declare it openly.

Less than a month before it had been the Thomas Committee that was in retreat. On October 30, 1947, at 3 p.m., in the middle of the proceedings and with many witnesses waiting to testify after traveling thousands of miles to be heard, the hearings were suddenly stopped. From the standpoint of J. Parnell Thomas the newspaper headlines and editorials and the radio comment had been something less than satisfactory. The current of adverse criticism was increasing in the responsible press. A deep-seated concern over civil liberties was stirring in the public consciousness. The report of the President's Commission on Civil Rights, presented in the midst of the hearings, served to emphasize even more sharply the Thomas Committee's denial of the American concept that a citizen shall have the right to hold what political opinions he pleases, and to hold them in the privacy of his own conscience.

So in the face of this cumulative massing of effective public opinion, J. Parnell Thomas rang down the curtain of his Washington-Hollywood extravaganza.

This was a tremendous victory for the representatives of the motion picture industry that had been so gratuitously attacked. It was greeted by adult public opinion, expressed by the *New York Times* and *Herald Tribune,* as a victory for the American people and the principles of good Americanism. It seemed to mark a turning in the high tide of hysteria. And it highlighted the failure of the Thomas Committee to meet the challenge of the Motion Picture Association spokesmen to name one picture tinged in the slighest degree with un-American propaganda.

In the midst of this victory the motion picture industry chose to reverse itself and embrace defeat. It chose to save the lost face of its persecutors and vilifiers, and to hand them their greatest triumph.

There is protocol in surrender designed to salve the pride of the defeated. In order to parley for terms, it is the custom to display a signal; a white flag, a white sheet, sometimes a white feather.

Five days before the simultaneous convening of the House of Representatives for the processing of the contempt citations and the gathering of the film producing clans, Eric Johnston made a well-publicized speech. During it he said:

"We did not defend them (the ten cited for contempt). We do not defend them now. On the contrary, we believe they have done a tremendous disservice to the industry which has given them so much material rewards and an opportunity to exercise their talents."

That was a remarkable statement; a smoke signal to those who had been waging a lurid campaign for federal censorship of the screen. The Hearst newspapers had been clamoring for what they called "rigid control" of the motion pictures. This was necessary, the Hearst editorialists argued, since the producers "had failed to clean their own house."

It mattered little that the Thomas Committee squirmed and

equivocated when challenged to point out, chapter and verse, where and in what film, Communist propaganda had been instilled.

It was a curious performance all around. It could have been compared to a boxing match in which the palpable winner is the one who suddenly throws in the sponge, whereupon the mystified spectators mutter, "Sellout!"

CHAPTER 23

"We do not ask you to condone this."[1]

THE details of the actual capitulation of the motion picture companies to the Thomas Committee and the ideological forces for which it played first fiddle, took place behind a velvet curtain of apprehensive secrecy. The press was barred and there was apparently an explicit understanding that none of the conferees would later reveal the processes of logic or its antithesis by which the great reversal had been achieved.

It is true that the two-day meeting ended with the release of a formal statement that the studios would "forthwith discharge or suspend without compensation" the ten men accused of being in contempt. But the authors of this decree were not sensitive to the stern compulsions which moved Thomas Jefferson and his collaborators in an earlier historic Declaration. No "decent respect to the opinions of mankind" seemed to require "that they should declare the causes which impel them to the separation."

Seventeen unrevealing words were considered enough to justify the new policy of the Motion Picture Association of America, which was also subscribed to by the theoretically autonomous Society of Independent Motion Picture Producers. They were black-listing the recalcitrant ten, they announced, because "their actions have been a disservice to their employers and have impaired their usefulness to the industry." The nature of the disservice was not explained nor was there a hint of how anyone could impair his usefulness by challenging the powers of the very committee which Johnston and McNutt had accused a few weeks earlier of attempted censorship and intimidation.

Speculation as to what went on behind those closed doors can only be based on the few facts at our disposal and the subsequent efforts of the chosen spokesmen of the group to rationalize their new and, in some cases, startlingly unfamiliar position.

The setting of the conference was one of the most handsome and expensive public rooms in the Waldorf-Astoria Hotel. It was the same room which has been on occasion graced by the governors of the National Association of Manufacturers and where it was determined what you shall pay for a gallon of gasoline, a carload of manganese, washing machine, or a roll of linoleum.

The cast of the drama included, of course, Eric Johnston, present in his capacity as president of the Motion Picture Association of America; James F. Byrnes and Paul V. McNutt, counsel for that organization; Barney Balaban, Nicholas Schenck, Harry Cohn, Joseph Schenck, J. Cheever Cowdin, Walter Wanger, Mendel Silberberg, Donald Nelson, Samuel Goldwyn, Y. Frank Freeman, Henry Ginsberg, Albert Warner, Louis B. Mayer, Dore Schary, Spyros Skouras, Nate Blumberg, William Goetz, Ned Depinet, and many more.

Some were star-characters and some supernumeraries. Some knew a great deal about what makes a motion picture and some knew nothing except that a film is something contained in flat tin cans which is supposed to yield a profit when exhibited to the public.

There were even one or two who were interested chiefly in how many tons of popcorn can be sold in the lobby while a particular picture is being unreeled.

But it is reasonable to assume that all of them, the devotees of prestige, profits, and popcorn alike, were aware that the gathering was a momentous one, for here, as the New York *Herald Tribune* detected, a precedent would be set: making political belief a test of employability. And among the conferees were some of the studio heads who had indignantly rejected the same plan when it had been urged upon them by the agents of the Thomas Committee in advance of the October hearings. Dore Schary of RKO-Radio had said categorically on the witness stand in Washington, when the Committee insisted he should fire any employee of whom they disapproved: "I would still maintain his right to think politically as he chooses."

It was here, in the words of the *Chicago Sun,* that the motion picture industry caved in and turned defeat into victory for J. Parnell Thomas, John Rankin, their colleagues, and supporters. But all we know is that the doors closed at eleven o'clock Monday morning and reopened early Tuesday afternoon to release a statement which should be examined in its entirety as part of our search for clues to the painful labor which precipitated its birth:

Members of the Association of Motion Picture Producers deplore the action of the ten Hollywood men who have been cited for contempt by the House of Representatives. We do not desire to prejudge their legal rights, but their actions have been a disservice to their employers and have impaired their usefulness to the industry.

We will forthwith discharge or suspend without compensation those in our employ, and we will not re-employ any of the ten until such time as he is acquitted, or has purged himself of contempt, and declared under oath that he is not a Communist.

On the broader issue of alleged subversive and disloyal elements in Hollywood, our members are likewise prepared to take positive action.

We will not knowingly employ a Communist or a member of any party or group which advocates the overthrow of the Government of the United States by force, or by any illegal or unconstitutional method.

In pursuing this policy, we are not going to be swayed by any hysteria or intimidation from any source.

We are frank to recognize that such a policy involves dangers and risks. There is the danger of hurting innocent people, there is the risk of creating an atmosphere of fear. Creative work at its best cannot be carried on in an atmosphere of fear. We will guard against this danger, this risk, this fear. To this end we will invite the Hollywood talent Guilds to work with us to eliminate any subversives; to protect the innocent, and to safeguard free speech and a free screen wherever threatened.

The absence of a national policy, established by Congress, with respect to the employment of Communists in private industry makes our task difficult. Ours is a nation of laws. We request Congress to enact legislation to assist American industry to rid itself of subversive, disloyal elements.

Nothing subversive or un-American has appeared on the screen, nor can any number of Hollywood investigations obscure the patriotic service of the 30,000 Americans employed in Hollywood who have given our Government invaluable aid in war and peace.

Two days later, when the news of the blacklist had been heard in every civilized quarter of the globe, the Screen Writers' Guild, whose members were most affected, received the following cryptogram:

IN THE INTEREST OF ALL OF US WE EARNESTLY SUG-GEST TO YOU THAT YOU JOIN WITH WALTER WANGER AND L. B. MAYER IN A MEETING AT MGM FRIDAY MORN-ING AT ELEVEN O'CLOCK STOP. WE SEEK TO ACQUAINT YOU WITH THE INTENT OF THE PRODUCERS' STATE-MENT AND TO REASSURE YOU THAT OUR ACTION IS DESIGNED, TO PROTECT THE INDUSTRY AND ALL THOSE ENGAGED IN IT AND TO DISAVOW ANY INTENTION OF A WITCH HUNT STOP. MAY WE URGE YOU AGAIN IN THE INTEREST OF ALL OF US TO WITHHOLD ANY ACTION STATEMENT OR COMMENT BY YOUR GUILD UNTIL WE HAVE MET AND EXCHANGED OUR VIEWS AND ATTITUDES STOP. THIS COMMITTEE ORGANIZED TO MEET WITH YOU INCLUDES L. B. MAYER, WALTER WANGER, DORE SCHARY, JOE SCHENCK AND HENRY GINSBERG AND WE ASK THAT YOU CONSIDER WHAT THESE MEN WANT TO SAY TO YOU BEFORE INDIVIDUAL GUILD ACTION IS DETERMINED OR BEFORE THE PRODUCERS ACTION IS MISUNDERSTOOD STOP. THANK YOU SINCERELY FOR YOUR COOPERATION. L. B. MAYER, CHAIRMAN, WALTER WANGER, JOE SCHENCK, HENRY GINSBERG, DORE SCHARY.

Representatives of the Screen Actors' and Screen Directors' Guilds were similarly summoned to the conclave. The studio heads had previously, in matters which couldn't be handled without the concurrence of the guilds, told them they were an essential part of The Industry and must participate in deciding policy. In this instance, the officers of the employee organizations suspected, their role was to be limited to accepting an accomplished fact, but they agreed nevertheless to withhold their judgment and listen.

It turned out they had quite a lot of listening to do. The first small meeting was followed by a larger one, to which the entire executive boards of the guilds were invited. Then, since no less an authority than the Thomas Committee had characterized the Screen Writers' Guild as the focal point of the infection its whole membership was assembled to hear the producers' committee.

It was generally agreed that Louis B. Mayer, at the second of these sessions, hit on the most graphic way of expressing the official point of view. The British people, he said, had their Royal Family, in the veneration of which a certain deep human impulse was satisfied. American democracy had to have a similar object of worship, and it had found it in the personalities of the motion picture business. That was why any word or act from Hollywood which shook the loyalty of even a fraction of the royal subjects was a matter for grave alarm and a potential contribution to national disintegration.

Mr. Mayer didn't have to labor the implications of his analogy. Hollywood glamor, for the purposes of his present definition, included the entire personnel of the studios, not just the stars whose images graced the household shrines of America. And it was an essential tradition of constitutional monarchy that the reigning sovereigns be above politics and refrain from any significant expression of opinion whatsoever.

The Guild representatives were affected by mixed emotions at this unexpected revelation. They were learning that there is no place of honor among mankind unaccompanied by sacrifice. They were being simultaneously enthroned and disfranchised.

But it was the statement of Doré Schary before the Writers' Guild of which he had once been a member, that was awaited with the greatest interest. For it was Schary who had answered back to Thomas and Stripling with the words "Up until the time it is proved that a Communist is a man dedicated to the overthrow of the government by force or violence, or by any illegal methods, I cannot make a determination of his employment on any other basis except whether he is qualified best to do the job I want him to do."

He had repeated his stand in other terms: "I will hire only those people I believe best qualified for their jobs until it is proven, until it is a matter of record and if that record is shown to me, of course I would not hire anyone who is dedicated to overthrow of the government by force." And he had explained in advance why these standards for dismissal did not apply to Adrian Scott and Edward Dmytryk, the two men his company subsequently dismissed: "I must say, not in defense but in honesty that at no time in discussions have I heard—or films— these men make any remark or attempt to get anything subversive into the films I have worked on with them. I must say that in honesty."

E. J. Mannix and Walter Wanger accompanied Schary to the writers' meeting—and left it without speaking a word. Schary was the spokesman and his colleagues were simply "present, as observers," apparently to see that the newly-minted executive talked like one instead of reverting to former type under the sinister influence of his erstwhile brethren.

Mr. Schary did not fail their expectations. The general impact of his extemporaneous speech was that the producers were opposed to the Thomas Committee, in fact despised it. They felt the freedom of the screen was in jeopardy. They were terribly sorry they had to fire anybody for any reason whatsoever, especially honest, talented people.

It was true that his own personal opinion had not been in accord with the determination of the New York meeting. That went for quite a few other producers, too. But in spite of their disagreement a unanimous decision had been reached to do exactly what the Thomas Committee had asked them to do. This was because the motion picture industry was very sensitive to public opinion. And any public opinion, even when it was manufactured by people out to control the thoughts and speech of American citizens, was still public opinion.

The producers had a threefold program, Mr. Schary told the writers. The first plank was to fire and blacklist the ten wit-

[187]

nesses. "We do not ask you to condone this," he assured an audience that included seven of the ten. Second was the policy of not hiring anyone *believed* to be a Communist. "We do not ask you to condone this," Mr. Schary repeated.

The third plank in the program was a big all-industry public relations campaign to restore the good name of Hollywood by convincing the American people that the first two planks were justified. This campaign, he was confident, the writers would not only condone but lend it their wholehearted support. Here the guilds and the producers could join in united action for the benefit of all.

As Mr. Schary descended the platform, Mr. Mannix and Mr. Wanger stood up to accompany him out. Sitting on the aisle in the front row was Dalton Trumbo. Many eyes watched this encounter between the would-be executioners and one of their principal victims. The three producers rose to the occasion. In turn they stopped, bent over, touched a friendly hand to Mr. Trumbo's slightly stiffened shoulder and spoke a word of greeting. Then they proceeded to leave the meeting, their gesture having demonstrated that the bonds of personal friendship transcended the unpleasant necessities of blacklist, career-wrecking, and character assassination.

The membership of the Screen Writers' Guild was so impressed by the Schary explanation that, with only eight dissenting votes, over four hundred men and women reaffirmed their decision to demand an end to the blacklist.

CHAPTER 24

"This is indeed most gratifying."

"NATURALLY, men scared to make pictures about the American Negro, men who only in the last year have allowed the word Jew to be spoken in a picture; men who took more than ten years to make an anti-fascist picture, those are frightened men," said Lillian Hellman, the celebrated playwright in *The Screen Writer* of December 1947.

"And you pick frightened men to frighten first," she continued. "Judas goats; they'll lead the others, maybe, to the slaughter. The others will be the radio, the press, the publishers, the trade unions, the colleges, the scientists, the churches —all of us. All of us who believe in this lovely land and its freedoms and rights, and who wish to keep it good and make it better."

So these frightened men meeting in the marble-paneled Waldorf-Astoria room crawled before the Thomas Committee they had at first defied, and asked to be forgiven.

J. Parnell Thomas, when he learned of this stunning victory, rubbed together his small, manicured hands, smiled his thin smile, and said: "This is indeed most gratifying."

It was commonly supposed that this surrender of the producers was the result of a deal. They would immolate on the altar of hysteria and reaction the ten top talent men who had challenged the right of a Congressional Committee to pry into their private beliefs. They would promise to purge other writers, directors, producers, and actors from the industry, and to ask Congress to pass a law telling them, as free entrepreneurs in a private enterprise economy exactly whom they could and could not hire. In return for all this, Thomas, it was assumed, would promise to call off any further investigation of Hollywood.

Such a deal may well have been made. If so, it must have been a shaky one. For Thomas, who has as little reason to trust the producers as they have to trust the headline-hunting Chairman of the Committee on Un-American Activities, soon began to speak threateningly of another Hollywood bread and circuses session for his Committee. He made little effort to hide his contempt for men who scuttled like so many rock crabs for cover under a camouflage of ringing platitudes. He said in an Associated Press interview: "Those Hollywood big shots were pretty high and mighty at first, but they got off their high horse, all right. Maybe after another lesson or two they will be able to run their industry on a safe, sound American basis."

If Mr. J. Parnell Thomas was slightly contemptuous and patronizing toward the men who so generously restored the face he had lost, the ordinary tub-thumpers for the Thomas Committee were far more open in their contempt.

"The death-bed repentance of Eric Johnston and his moving picture magnates may take some of the curse off them at the box office, but it isn't going to stop the investigation of their industry," said the *Chicago Tribune* as: "The producers were in such a hurry to get right with their life-giving public that they cast the ten Communists into the outer darkness without even waiting for them to be convicted."

Said Westbrook Pegler in his Hearst newspaper column: "They did not proceed against these ten until the industry had been dragged in legirons and handcuffs, so to speak, before the Committee. The agents of the industry tried to ridicule the Committee but the fact got across to the people that his Committee represented and actually personified them. . . . All at once the men who represented the industry stopped short and went into a solemn frightened huddle in New York."

George E. Sokolsky, writing in the *Washington Times-Herald* of Dec. 1, 1947, said that in spite of the position taken by Eric Johnston and Paul McNutt at the hearings that the industry was pure and would not resort to a blacklist, the industry itself took two important steps which he felt constrained to praise: It purged itself of radical control within the Screen Writers' Guild, and it sent its leading moguls to the Waldorf-Astoria to announce the firing of those accused of contempt for the Thomas Committee and its procedures.

The Los Angeles *Times* said in a leading editorial: "Eric Johnston has a disconcerting change of pace, but uncertain control, and experience tells the batter that he can never know where the President of the Motion Picture Association is going to throw the next one. A few weeks ago Mr. Johnston was chiding the Committee on Un-American Activities for smearing Hollywood. . . . Now, less than a month later, Mr. Johnston issues a statement in New York which will surprise the members of the Thomas Committee and quite a few Americans who are not in Congress. Of the ten witnesses who refused to avow or disavow Communism, he says, 'Their refusal to stand up and be counted resulted in confusion of the issues before the Committee.' But it will seem to those who read Mr. Johnston's full page newspaper advertisements and his statement to the Committee that his own contribution to the confusion has been substantial. First the Committee was wrong in questioning the witnesses; then the witnesses were wrong in not answering the question."

Hundreds of newspapers and commentators less friendly to the Thomas Committee and to the industry, were far more candid in their opinions of the switch engineered at the Waldorf-Astoria. If it was better public relations and understanding that Mr. Johnston and his associates sought, their success was less than brilliant.

In the meantime the producers carried through their terms of surrender to the Thomas Committee. They fired Adrian Scott, producer; Edward Dmytryk, director; Lester Cole, Ring Lardner, Jr., and Dalton Trumbo, writers; and they placed on an open blacklist John Howard Lawson, Albert Maltz, Alvah Bessie, Samuel Ornitz, and Herbert Biberman.

In firing Scott and Dmytryk, the RKO letter said: "By your conduct (in refusing to answer questions) and by your actions, attitude, public statements, and general conduct before, at and since that time, you have brought yourself into disrepute with large sections of the public, have offended the community, have prejudiced this corporation as your employer and the motion picture industry in general, have lessened your capacity fully to comply with your employment agreement, and have otherwise violated your employment agreement with us."

In a joint statement concerning their position after indictment Scott and Dmytryk said: "As a footnote to the perversion of justice, history will record the temporary triumph of John Rankin of Mississippi who in the halls of Congress brought the citation debate to an end with a calculated anti-Semitic reference. We feel that *Crossfire* will stand as testament to our Americanism long after Rankin and Thomas are dead."

A postlude to the action of the producers in instituting a blacklist and breaking contracts was recorded in Philadelphia on December 4, 1947, just ten days after the producers had announced that Adrian Scott, Edward Dmytryk, and eight other men would be fired or blacklisted.

In the historic City of Brothery Love, the old Golden Slipper Square Club had presented its award to the film *Crossfire* for its great contribution to the cause of tolerance. Adrian Scott was the producer of this film. Edward Dmytryk was its director. Together they had conceived and nurtured the project of making it. Dore Schary, executive head of the RKO studio where the picture was made, was invited to Philadelphia to receive the award. He made his excuses. But Eric Johnston was not abashed.

The men who presided over the meeting where the producer and director of *Crossfire* were fired for insisting on the right of privacy for personal beliefs went to Philadelphia, accepted the award, and made a speech about the beauties of tolerance. Hollywood, he said, must be eternally vigilant against all forms of intolerance. Making pictures, he said, is a big job, and intolerance can set up restrictions and barriers interfering with the kind of true creative effort that produced *Crossfire*. He gave expression to his pride that Hollywood held wide the door of opportunity to every man and woman who could meet its technical and artistic requirements, regardless of racial background or beliefs.

The reporters did not record whether or not Mr. Johnston blushed when he said it, but blushes must have incarnadined many a Hollywood cheek when his remarks were read.

CHAPTER 25

"This action was engineered by the industry's overlords."

HOLLYWOOD has always been beset by fears. Its golden rewards have been so sudden and so lush for the owners and top executives of the motion picture industry that they shiver timidly at the least breath of criticism. The industry submits with hardly a token resistance to the dubiously legal state and city censorship boards which push it around. It has habitually quailed before all kinds of organized pressure groups, and sought to appease them in any way that will still allow it to make a profit.

It has succumbed to almost every form of pressure—except the pressure to make a greater proportion of intelligent pictures that will help attract to the box office a large segment of the adult population that now refrains from the movie habit.

But it is doubtful in the extreme that it was the pressure of public opinion, the desire for better public relations, that made the industry succumb to the Thomas Committee and reverse the positions taken by its own representatives at the hearing. For in this case the weight of public opinion was clearly against the methods of the Thomas Committee, and in favor of the contention that the test of the Committee's charges was in the pictures and that no disloyal or subversive picture had ever been made.

What, then, caused the sudden switch?

Ed Sullivan, gossip column conductor for the *New York Daily News,* a sworn editorial foe of the purge victims got this succinct explanation past the copy desk on November 29: "Reason that Hollywood big shots rushed to New York and barred the ten cited by Congress: Hollywood has been dealt a blow that won't please Wall Street financiers, who have millions invested in picture companies. Wall Street jiggled the strings, that's all."

Bosley Crowther, in the *New York Times* on December 7 said the same thing in more cultured terms: "It should be fully realized that this action (capitulation to Thomas Committee) was engineered by the major New York executives, the industry's overlords, and not by the 'Hollywood producers', who form a different and subordinate group."

There can be no doubt that Bosley Crowther, Ed Sullivan, and many other informed observers are correct in their statement that the retreat of the producers was dictated from above —from the great banks, holding corporations, insurance companies that form the financial complex that controls the motion picture industry. The industry is interlocked inextricably with international big business. Those in real control of motion pictures—in their raw materials, patent rights, studio equipment, exhibition space, and financing are principally interested in power and profits, and in the expansion of power and profits.

So the Hollywood producers and their lawyers and advisors got word from their real bosses to reverse their position about Mr. Thomas and his Committee; the frightened men at the Waldorf-Astoria were not fearful of bad public relations—they were fearful about the jobs that pay them from $100,000 to $1,000,000 a year. If one has to jump through a hoop or do a quick-change act once in a while to hold that kind of a job, well, it is worth it.

For some idea of the interlocking financial set-up of the motion picture companies, look at Moody's Index of corporate ownership and control. You will find that Columbia is interlocked with some of the great international banking firms of Europe and America; that Paramount control is mixed up with banks, oil, Coca Cola, power, copper, rubber, and motor cars; that MGM is intricately associated with great investment trusts and power corporations; that RKO is not a stranger to Atlas Corporation, United Fruit, National Can; that 20th Century-Fox is scrambled with General Foods, Pan-American Airways, New York Trust, National Distillers; that Warner Bros. has affiliation with J. P. Morgan & Co. and American Power & Light; that

[195]

Universal is hooked up with the vast ramifications of the J. Arthur Rank interests and involved in the securities portfolio of J. Cheever Cowdin.

The film industry, which speaks in the international language of pictures, is a major opinion-forming agency not only here in America, but in Latin America, Europe, Asia, and Africa.

The real controlling interests of this industry are not so much interested in the freedom and creativeness of the motion pictures. They are interested first in making money from films. But they are also interested, and perhaps increasingly so, in using films both as a medium to protect their privileges and their plans for expanded markets, and as a soporific or escape valve for people who might otherwise read or think at home, or talk over high prices and what to do about them with neighbors or fellow-workers.

These real owners and controllers of the motion picture industry may be frightened men, too. They are frightened of change and their fear is a cold, calculated fear. In the light of this basic motivation, the so-called retreat of the motion-picture industry is not a retreat at all, but a ruthless, aggressive advance, against all that the people want and expect of Americanism and democracy.

CHAPTER 26

"My opinion is that if (the question) reached the Supreme Court, the so-called unfriendly witnesses would be vindicated."

THE task of restoring lost face to the Motion Picture Municheers proved too much even for the publicity organs of the industry working under full throttle. Thousands of line-inches of newspaper copy and typhoons of oratory appeared to move nobody to support of the producers' position—least of all in Hollywood. Indeed, the stain of pusilanimity, like Lady Macbeth's "damn'd spot" would not come out.

The great majority of the 32,000 men and women engaged in making America's films recognized that none of them—not one —is exempt from the blacklist which was uttered as anathema upon the "unfriendly" witnesses. One guild leader warned: "Get set for a new $64 question. It's going to run like this: 'Are you a loyal American worker, or will you resist a wage-cut, you dirty red!'"

And elsewhere in America, intelligent newspaper readers became aware of another phenomenon that developed in the Caucus Room in Washington. It had become clear that there was a double-standard of public morality—one for the free-enterprising film companies and another for the ten free-enterprisers who chose to meet the Thomas Committee's challenge on their feet.

Which can come before the court of public opinion with clean hands? The ten companies or the ten cited witnesses?

The heads of the studios who knuckled under, pleading pressure by their boards of directors and their stockholders? Or, the ten men who invoked (when they were allowed) their dignity as artists, as citizens and as men, the Constitution of the United States, and the American tradition?

In the hearing room these men were painted as some species of voluptuaries. Inspired press descriptions made them intellectual sprites on some Hollywood Olympus, lolling beside swimming pools filled with Chanel No. 5 while bonded messengers brought them their $2,000 to $5,000 pay checks, each week out of the 52, on the dot.

This picture of the men, sketched by J. Parnell Thomas, his legislative colleagues and the "friendly" witnesses, is crudely and calculatedly false. The fact is there isn't a swimming pool among the ten. Their salaries, even where $2,000 a week obtained were earned stipend—and not the year 'round, either. No studio ever maintained a writer on its payroll if his work didn't fetch a profit.

True, they did not receive pittances and some had substantial savings. But when the subpoenas arrived for them from Washington, it was the equivalent of a sight-draft on the men's fortunes. What happened thereafter is that men have been punished for a crime that does not exist. As E. B. White pointed out in the *New Yorker:* "Ten men have been convicted, not of wrong-doing but of wrong thinking; that is news in this country and if I have not misread my history, it is bad news."

There was, in fact, bad news for all decent Americans in every delivery of mail to the ten "unfriendly" witnesses during the time they were under subpoena in Washington. Every day a clerk of the Thomas Committee delivered to them batches of postal cards and letters addressed care of the Committee. Nine out of ten were scurrilous. Some used the word "Jew" as an epithet. Others called the witnesses "kikes," "nigger lovers" and other terms unprintable though less obscene. If such scurrility had been sent through the mail to producers, the FBI would be beating the bushes for the senders.

Some well intentioned and honestly curious have continued to demand of the "unfriendly" witnesses a statement of their union and political affiliations. The "friendly" witnesses left no such doubts, the argument runs. They made themselves quite clear. The Sam Woods, the Menjous, the Taylors, and the Macauleys expatiated on their political inclinations. They were given all the time they needed. As for the ten, the statements that would have expressed their beliefs just as clearly were rejected by the Thomas Committee.

The New York *Herald Tribune* put to Ring Lardner, Jr., a series of questions covering the points on which J. Parnell Thomas demanded "Yes," or "No," as the only answers that would satisfy him.

It should be recognized here that the *Herald Tribune,* the leading Republican newspaper of the nation, has shown an intelligent awareness of the dangers inherent in the Thomas committee's abuse of power. It has spoken up vigorously on the side of civil liberties. In answering these questions, Lardner permitted the other nine men who had been cited for contempt of the Committee to see them. They all agreed that his answers would have been theirs as well.

The pertinent questions and Lardner's answers were:

Are you a member of the Screen Writers' Guild?

Ten years ago it could, and sometimes did, mean the loss of a screen writer's job to admit membership in the guild. There are plenty of signs in Hollywood and in the country as a whole to indicate we may face such a period of terror again. I believe the right of a union to secrecy of its membership lists and the right of an individual employee to keep his union affiliations to himself are basic rights. It happens, however, that the Thomas Committee didn't have to cite me for contempt to gain this information. They could have found their answer by reading the guild stationery or the guild magazine, in both of which places I was listed as a member of the executive board. It is a matter of similarly public record that I have been treasurer and a vice-president of the organization.

Are you, or have you ever been a member of the Communist Party?

I do not wish to answer this question at this time for what seems to me to be cogent and compelling reasons. They are based on my conviction that the right to hold any political belief, including that of Communism, carries with it, as a natural corollary, the right to choose for oneself the time and occasion to make a public statement of one's opinions. I do not care for the idea of answering under pres-

[199]

sure questions which are traditionally and Constitutionally my own business.

The pressure in regard to this particular question began when I received a subpoena from the Un-American Activities Committee last September, and will continue, according to the way I see it, until Congress and the courts restore for our generation the Jeffersonian concept of free opinion, speech and political affiliation.

Since my appearance at the Thomas Committee hearings in October, the motion-picture companies have announced a policy of intimidation which makes it even more distasteful for me to reply to the question and even more romantic to pretend that such a reply would be a voluntary one.

As the question stands now, if I am a member of the Communist Party I would be exposing myself to the bigotry and inspired hysteria which is forcing not only the Communists but all Left-of-Center political groups into a semi-secret status. More specifically, in view of the Motion Picture Association's blacklist statement, I would be banishing myself permanently from the profession in which I have earned my living since I was twenty-one.

If I am not a member, I would be exposing other men to the same bigotry and blacklist by contributing to the precedent that all non-Communists must so declare themselves in order to isolate the actual offenders. Further, it would be clear to every one, including me, that I had purged myself in order to please my past and prospective employers.

I realize that much of the opposition to those of us who challenged the Thomas Committee's powers is based on the theory that Communists are advocates of terror and violence, or foreign agents, or both. But the Supreme Court determined in the Schneiderman decision that this was not the case. And even if it has become so since, acts of treason must be uncovered and punished by due and orderly process of law.

The Communists declare themselves to be loyal Americans, and they propagandize in favor of democracy, tolerance, and higher living standards. Their critics say they don't really believe in these things.

I'm not trying to prove here which side of the argument is right. I simply maintain that it is not sound Americanism to prosecute or persecute people for what they think or what we think they think.

[200]

Only an act can be a crime, never an idea. As Jefferson put it. "It is time enough for the rightful purposes of civil government for its officers to interfere when principles break out into overt acts against peace and good order."

I am withholding my answer at this moment, then, because I am in the middle of a fight for my right to keep silent about my political beliefs. This is exactly the same right that is protected by the secret ballot or, as Alvah Bessie pointed out on the witness stand, that General Eisenhower was tacitly invoking when people were still wondering whether he was a Republican or a Democrat. Freedom of speech has no practical reality unless it includes the freedom to associate and act in concert with others of a like mind, and the freedom to keep to himself those opinions and associations a man doesn't feel ready to communicate to his neighbor.

*Why did you refuse to answer these questions when
they were asked by the House Un-American Activities
Committee?*

I am not quibbling but speaking the literal truth when I say that I did not refuse to answer any question. The transcript shows that I was interrupted every time I started to speak, sometimes after only one or two words. What I did do was refuse to submit to a yes-or-no limitation after the Committee had given its "friendly" witnesses absolute latitude, including the right to make statements ten times as long and one-tenth as pertinent as the one I was refused permission to make.

I took this position for two reasons. One, as I have explained in relation to your previous questions, was that I wanted to tell the Committee that no one has to reveal what trade union or political party he belongs to, and the greater the display of force, the more I feel impelled to make this a part of my answer.

The second reason was that I hate the purposes and methods of men like Thomas and Rankin, and I wanted in the course of my answer to challenge their Committee at the very foundation of its existence: its asserted power to enforce answers in violation of the Bill of Rights.

I have always favored a broad interpretation of the powers of the legislative branch of the government and I have a sincere respect for the function and historic accomplishments of Congressional investigating committees. But I believe they are required to operate within the broad purpose of gathering information which might be the basis of new legislation. During its ten years of existence the Un-American Activities Committee has only proposed one piece of legislation, and that was declared unconstitutional. The law at which they said they were aiming in this case was one outlawing the Communist Party. But Congress has no right to declare a person or group of persons illegal by name. It can only legislate general principles and standards so that people and parties that violate them can then be prosecuted.

The real purpose of the hearings was clearly exposed when the Committee told the producers what kind of pictures to make and whom to hire and fire. That does not fall within the widest possible interpretation of what an investigating Committee is supposed to do.

Do you dispute or accept the authenticity of testimony giving the number of a Communist Party card and stating that it was issued to you?

To do either would be contrary to the position I have taken in answer to your second question. But I think the Committee's shy reluctance to let any witness, lawyer or newspaperman get a glimpse of its "evidence" speaks for itself. And I would like to say that the one feature of the hearings which wounded me more than any other was the accusation that I, as a man supposedly making his living by his imagination, would conceal my identity under the pseudonym of "Ring L."

The other point in regard to these "party cards" has been called to my attention since the hearings. I think it is interesting because it shows how careless an "investigator" can get when working for a committee which considers itself bound by no law or customary rules of procedure. All of the cards introduced into the record were allegedly issued in November or December, 1944, to cover the year 1945. Mr. Russell, the investigator, claimed to be reading from the documents as he spoke. In each case he described his find as a "Communist party registration card."

Yet for some six months before and after those dates there was no Communist Party of the United States in existence. The organization had been dissolved and a new one founded under the name of the

Communist Political Association. Whether that change of name represented a technicality or an actuality is beside the point. Obviously the Communists themselves must have taken it seriously enough to alter their official documents.

But all these points are, I will admit, more amusing than they are relevant. What really matters is that this sort of testimony, based on one man's word without any mention of where and how he obtained his information, has no legal validity whatsoever. It is a very dangerous precedent when a government body without any judicial function assumes one and still claims it is not subject to any rules of judicial procedure.

If I am accused of a crime under the law and admissable evidence is presented against me, I can confirm or deny it. If I refuse to do so, the jury can draw its own conclusions. But if a man claiming to be a police officer enters my house without a warrant and says, "We were tapping your phone the other night and we heard you say some things that sounded pretty dangerously like Episcopalianism," I will feel much more obligated to comment on the man than on his evidence against me.

Though Ring Lardner, Jr.'s statements add to clarity of the stand taken by himself and his colleagues in the public mind, one noted constitutional authority understood it earlier and clearly enough to predict the consequences of their behavior. Thurman Arnold, former special assistant to the United States Attorney General pointed out that as a question of Constitutional law, it is not pertinent whether or not the ten witnesses were "evading" the issue of their union or political affiliations. He added:

"In order to test the constitutional right of any Congressional committee to ask such questions as: 'Are you a member of the Screen Writers' Guild?' and 'Are you now or have you ever been a member of the Communist Party?' it was necessary for these witnesses to do three things:

"1. Phrase their answers as they did;

"2. Accept citations for contempt of Congress;

"3. Stand trial in the Federal courts, and if convicted of contempt appeal to the Supreme Court of the United States.

"Only in this way can the question of Constitutional law involved be clarified, and precedent established. My opinion is that if it reached the Supreme Court, the so-called unfriendly witnesses would be vindicated."

But it is a costly road that leads to the Supreme Court and vindication.

What price liberty in 1948? What price civil rights? Or freedom? It is possible, if the price is too dear, to buy another, less expensive kind?

One great American, Wendell Willkie, who saw survival for mankind as one people in one world, didn't think so. He said, "Freedom is indivisible; and you can't have one kind of freedom for the rich and another for the poor; one kind of freedom for the opinions of the majority and another kind of freedom for the opinions of the minority."

CHAPTER 27

> "If this (the activity of the Thomas Committee)
> is legally permissible, it can be asserted dog-
> matically that investigation of private opinion
> is not really prohibited under the Bill of
> Rights."

IT has been a long story, and we, of Hollywood, who put it
together modestly assert that it has some of the basic elements
of the kind of literature that reflects its time.

There is conflict—the conflict of liberal, Jeffersonian democracy at grips with something new and mongrel in America. It
has, too, something of the spy-thriller, its blacklegs and informers. There is suspense. There is a beginning. There is a middle.

As for an end—the kind of end that ties up every loose string
of the narrative and answers every question posed—the reader
will have to look away from the book to the tide of America's
aspiration for liberty and full freedom.

Today it is at ebb. For these reasons:

A major assault against the mass agencies of public opinion,
culture and entertainment has for the time succeeded.

The time, place and particular salient had been shrewdly
chosen. It was a full panoplied attack against the Maginot Line
of the communications institutions—the films. The terms were
unconditional surrender of those who control the industry, the
generals. But the subjugation of the people who work in it has
not yet been achieved. *They* are still fighting.

For the first time since labor rose to its earned dignity as the
prime factor in America's growth, a political blacklist was established in defiance of specific laws against it.

A trend toward honesty and courage in motion pictures, the
principal entertainment medium of America's 140,000,000 peo-

ple, was stopped at a point where it had begun to be esteemed the world over.

Creative men and women in the motion picture industry were given notice that the talents they had hired out to their employers were strictly under control, and that there could be no free creative endeavor.

A motion picture censorship was set up, tailored to the William Randolph Hearst standards.

The motion picture industry was put on notice, co-ordinated, so to speak, for the job of softening, confusing and conditioning the American mind for reaction.

A powerful impetus toward company unionism was set up. Not more than a few days after the films' capitulation an "independent" union offered itself to replace the present employees of the make-up departments, pledging to work longer hours for less money.

Most important of all, a dangerous breach was made in the Bill of Rights—a shield that for 150 years has protected the freedom of opinion and conscience in America.

Yet all this was not done by executive fiat as in a totalitarian country, but by an investigating committee of Congress—a fraction of the legislative arm of government.

Thomas Jefferson warned of this arrogance of the legislative. In a letter to James Madison, on March 15, 1789, he wrote: "The executive power in our government is not the only, perhaps not even the principal object of my solicitude. The tyranny of the legislature is really the danger most to be feared, and will continue to be so for many years to come. The tyranny of the executive power will come in its turn, but at a more distant period."

But, between the legislature and the executive stands the judiciary and here the outlook is not without encouragement to those who cherish the traditions of our land.

The Supreme Court has not yet spoken on the issue of civil liberties which stem out of the Thomas Committee. An inferior court, however, has reviewed a conviction for contempt in the case of Leon Josephson, a New York attorney who challenged the constitutionality of the Thomas Committee and its right to question him.

The decision in the United States Circuit Court of Appeals upheld Josephson's conviction by a two-to-one decision. But the dissenting opinion by United States Judge Charles E. Clark, renowned for his studies in constitutional law, was rendered with great vigor and scholarship. It is now being quoted and seriously studied throughout the nation. It was distinctly not good news to J. Parnell Thomas.

In an opinion following the precedents of the late Justice Holmes and within the great tradition of Franklin D. Roosevelt, Judge Clark hammered home the considered opinion that the House Committee on Un-American Activities has repeatedly and illegally misused its power and subverted the Constitution. He pointed out that continuation of these illegal acts must seriously jeopardize American liberties.

He challenged sharply the constitutionality of the House of Representatives resolution setting up the Dies-Rankin-Thomas Committee. Judge Clark did this on the ground that Congressional committees are not empowered in the exercise of their investigating function to do what would be unconstitutional if done in exercise of the legislative function.

Judge Clark quoted prior determining decisions that neither House of Congress has the general power to inquire into private affairs and beliefs, and to compel disclosures. He said:

"If this (the activity of the Thomas Committee) is legally permissible, it can be asserted dogmatically that investigation of private opinion is not really prohibited under the Bill of Rights. In other words, there will have been discovered a blank spot in the protective covering of that venerated document."

He pointed out that "while the power of inquiry is an essential and appropriate auxiliary to the legislative function, it must be exerted with due regard for the rights of witnesses, and a witness rightfully may refuse to answer where the bounds of the power are exceeded or where the questions asked are not pertinent to the matter under inquiry."

In this arresting opinion much consideration was given to the vagueness of the term *un-American*. Judge Clark observed that the most concrete and usual definition of un-Americanism was the advocacy of opinions and policies at variance with those of giant industrial organizations concerning what they like to call "the American Way" or the "American theory of free enterprise."

"As a matter of fact," said the federal judge, "the testimony at the recent movie investigation found the necessary un-American qualities for which the committee was searching in films which placed bankers in an unfavorable light or talked against the free enterprise system."

And further: "The (Thomas) Committee announces its desire that the persons it finds guilty shall forfeit their jobs in public and private industry and shall be subject to prosecution for any collateral crimes which may have been disclosed, and generally shall be exposed pitilessly to public condemnation. There can be no doubt of the obvious and direct abridgment of the right freely to speak and express one's opinions which is thus achieved."

In a summary of the dubious actions of the Thomas Committee, the opinion continued, "It invites and justifies an attempt to enforce conformity of political thinking, to penalize the new and the original, to label as subversive or un-American the attempt to devise new approaches for the public welfare—in short, to damn that very kind of initiative in experimentation which has made our democracy grow and flourish."

Judge Clark's opinion is one of the most authoritative challenges yet made to the Thomas Committee. It is buttressed with precedents from prior court decisions and will undoubtedly have an impact in the determination of subsequent cases.

As in no other case in our times, the issue of civil liberties and its possible future aspect was posed here, in this account. The press and radio recognition of the events in Washington from October 20 to 30, 1947, has been unprecedented. Its effect on other nations was profound. There they commented that the freedom from fear advocated by Franklin D. Roosevelt is changing in America to a fear of freedom. There they watch intently to see how far a nation that *talks* of democracy, individual rights and peace, *acts* in advocacy of these same freedoms.

The showdown cannot be far ahead. Events are moving with the speed of jet-propulsion these days.

We have seen the pattern of a mental straitjacket; police opinion in a policed state. We are being invited to try it on—just for size.

We must reject it, in the name of the America that we have always known and the liberty our children have a right to inherit from us.

The alternative is hardly conceivable.

A POST SCRIPT

THE protagonist in this narrative—the ten who stood upon their rights under the Constitution of the United States in their challenge to the House Un-American Activities Committee, and who, at the instance of that Committee were indicted for contempt, present an Un-Americanism Quiz of their own devising.

Here then is a Litmus Test of Loyalty—a Ready Political Reckoner by which the reader may determine whether he is an American in the terms of Franklin D. Roosevelt or J. Parnell Thomas.

CAUTION! These questions are loaded. Do not handle unless experienced in the use of explosives. Avoid proximity to children and open fires.

INSTRUCTIONS

Score yourself 5 points for each time you answer "Yes."
You will be rated according to the following schedule

40 to 50—Suspicious
50 to 60—Under Scrutiny
60 to 70—Definite Security Risk
70 to 80—Confirmed Fellow-Traveler
80 to 90—National Menace
90 to 100—Subpoena En route

A score of under 30 means you have no cause for alarm except the normal hazards of cave-dwelling. When played by two, oral answers may be given in whispers, preferably outdoors, in areas cleared of vegetation and microphones. Contestants who put their answers in writing are urged to do so on cigarette papers which may be rolled up and easily swallowed.

1. Do you find yourself wondering what the Thomas Committee may think of some of your opinions on:
   Jim Crow. Anti-Semitism. High Prices. The Taft-Hartley Act. Your Landlord.

2. Can it be said that you ever committed any of these sins cited as proof of subversive activity against the Hollywood witnesses:

   Questioned American foreign policy.
   Urged the U. S. to sever diplomatic relations with Spain. Defended the rights of the foreign-born. ———

3. Does it affect your national pride to hear that England has offered sanctuary to political refugees from the American Motion Picture Industry? ———

4. Do you worry about what the Thomas Committee's thought-control program will mean to:

   Education. Science. Labor. The newspapers and radio. ———

5. Do you think that what the movies need is more resemblance to real life, rather than less? ———

6. Are you a Jew or a Catholic? A member of a racial or national minority? Are you a trade unionist? A Mason? Of foreign descent? ———

7. Do you subscribe to any magazine or newspaper containing ideas not endorsed by the National Association of Manufacturers? ———

8. Are there any books in your shelves it might be more discreet to put away in a cupboard? Or in an incinerator? ———

9. Do you brood about the kind of world your children are going to live in? ———

10. Have you begun to worry about what it's safe to say over the telephone? Do you sometimes hear a strange click when you pick it up? ———

11. Does it seem possible to you that there can ever be a blacklist in your own profession, shop or business? ———

12. Do you still think a man's loyalty should be judged by his acts, when it is so much more convenient to indict him for what somebody thinks are his thoughts? ———

13. Are you a political fundamentalist? In other words, do you take the Declaration of Independence and The Constitution literally instead of recognizing that they are just great examples of allegorical writing, suitable for chants? ———

14. Did you oppose fascism before the period in which it was fashionable to do so? Or since?   ————

15. Do you ever question what you read in *Life* magazine?   ————

16. Do you give a damn about what people in other countries think about us?   ————

17. Did you ever have any friends with Russian names? Eat Russian dressing? Sing a Russian lullaby? Play Russian Bank?   ————

18. Have you forgotten what you meant when you said what you did to that fellow in the gas station that time?   ————

19. Would you rather answer questions like this voluntarily than have J. Parnell Thomas threaten you with a jail sentence if he didn't like what you said?   ————

20. Do you believe the 81st Congress can get along with one less committee than the 80th?   ————

YOUR SCORE   ————

STATEMENTS

JUDY GARLAND said:

Before every free conscience in America is subpoenaed, please speak up! Say your piece. Write your Congressman a letter! Airmail special! Let the Congress know what you think of its Un-American Committee. Tell them how much you resent the way Mr. Thomas is kicking the living daylights out of the Bill of Rights!

GEORGE S. KAUFMAN said:

We have seen the beginning of a shabby melodrama, with Mr. Thomas playing the part of the prompter. But in American life we need no prompter. So far this first phase has been an indecent tragedy of fear. We must see to it that this Un-American spectacle does not become a continuous performance.

FRANK KINGDON, Radio Commentator and Columnist, N. Y. Post, said:

The capitulation of the Motion Picture Association to the Thomas Committee's assault upon a free screen in America and upon the basic rights of workers in the motion picture industry is an act so shameful and so fraught with danger as to call for an all out resistance by freedom loving Americans everywhere.

SWEDEN'S MOST DISTINGUISHED ACTORS AND DIRECTORS in a statement delivered to the U. S. Legation in Stockholm:

With great amazement and consternation we, the undersigned Swedish actors and directors, have heard of the action taken by the Un-American Committee against some of our colleagues. Amazement that such an action, a denial of all democratic rights, should occur in that land in which the Declaration of Rights was born; consternation at the existence of a mentality which would deny a free artist his right to his personal, private opinion.

It is our wish that this protest and declaration of sympathy for the accused shall be delivered, through the Ambassador, to the American press and to all those of our colleagues who are affected by this action.

> *Signed:* Maria Schildknecht Wahlgren, Karin Kavli, Kerstin Rabe, Kolbjorn Knudsen, Anders Ek, Ulf Johansson, Gunn Wallgren, Ulla Sallert, Torsten Bergstrom, Carl Reinholdz, Ake Soderblom, Willy Peters, George Fant, Hampe Faustman, Gun Robertson, Ragnvi Lindblad, Per Hjern, Olle Florin, Bengt Ekerot, Erik Strandmark, Carl Hugo Calander, Bengt Brunskog and Elsa Widborg.

FREDRIC MARCH said:

Who do you think they're really after? Who's next? Is it your minister who will be told what he can say in his pulpit? Is it your children's school teacher who will be told what she can say in classrooms? Is it your children themselves? It is you, who will have to look around nervously before you say what is on your mind? Who are they after? They're after more than Hollywood. This reaches into every American city and town.

SENATOR GLEN TAYLOR said:

I'm from Idaho. The folks from my state don't like anyone to put fences around our thinking. I'm climbing on a horse this afternoon . . . and I'm going to ride. I want to get the attention of the people. I know that the penalty for doing your own thinking nowadays is to be labelled red. But I think it's time for somebody to speak up for peace and while I'm doing that I intend to battle this Un-American Committee to a standstill. Americans have always been able to speak out free and easy . . . whether it's on celluloid or on your own front porch. As a United States Senator, I want to see that it stays that way!

SENATOR ALBERT THOMAS OF UTAH said:

To me the Constitution of the United States is a sacred document. The rights and privileges it guarantees are sacred and I label as unholy the methods adopted by the House Un-American Activities Committee in pursuing its course of trying to establish arbitrary values of Americanism. If these men be guilty of subversive activity, let the evidence be presented and their guilt duly established, but at all cost we must avoid persecution in the name of investigation.

CORNEL WILDE said:

Another man who doesn't like the Committee is Scripps Howard columnist and Pulitzer Prize winner, Thomas L. Stokes. He said that the investigation had the ring of hypocrisy. He added:

The inquisition becomes the concern of everybody who believes in freedom of expression in writing and the arts. Moreover, the fright technique has been chosen for this job. It does all seem confused and quite strange to be happening here.

GREGORY PECK said:

There is more than one way to lose your liberty. It can be torn out of your hands by a tyrant—but it can also slip away, day by day, while you're too busy to notice, or too confused, or too scared.

JAMES IMBRIE, chairman Trenton, N. J., Independent Citizens League, said:

Our group thoroughly condemns Hollywoods' bootlicking of Un-American Committee. We are with you in fight against vicious blacklists and goosestep censorship. Jersey liberals personally disgraced by Parnell Thomas. Will do our best to evict him from Congress.

BENNETT CERF said:

If Hollywood can be bullied into producing only the kind of stories that fall in with this Committee's opinions and prejudices, it seems obvious to me that the publishers of books, magazines, and newspapers will most certainly be next on the agenda.

SENATOR HARRY KILGORE of WEST VIRGINIA said:

I'd like to say a word about Congressional investigations. I've had a hand in one or two myself, and I know how they work. . . . There are lots of ways of running the show, you can ask questions because you want answers or you can ask questions because you don't want answers. You can walk into the hearing with a bucket of whitewash, or a barrel of red paint. You can call a man any name and accuse him of anything, without being sued for libel and without fear of him answering back. Think of that when you read the papers these days. Remember—it's easy to splash red paint on someone . . . and it's pretty tough to wipe it off.

LUCILLE BALL said:

All of us agree that the Constitution of the United States must be defended! But the way to do this is not by shutting up the man you disagree with; you must fight for his right to speak and be heard. All civil liberties go hand in hand, and when one goes the others are weakened, just as the collapse of one pillar in a house would endanger the whole structure.

BURT LANCASTER said:

Gerald L. K. Smith says, *Be sure to write a letter to Congressman John Rankin, congratulating him and his committee.*

Who is Gerald L. K. Smith? A rabble-rouser, a professional anti-Semite, and one-time speaker for the German-American Bund.

ROBERT RYAN said:

President Roosevelt called the Un-American Committee *A sordid procedure* and that describes it pretty accurately. Decent people dragged through the mud of insinuation and slander. The testimony of crackpots and subversives accepted and given out to the press as if it were gospel truth. Reputations ruined and people hounded out of their jobs.

JOHN GARFIELD said:

There is no guarantee that the Committee will stop with movies. Already the American theatre, which I love, has been attacked. Already a witness friendly to the Committee has assured us that 44 per cent of the plays on Broadway in the last ten years have been subversive. That's news to Broadway, and to the millions of playgoers who have seen these plays.

MYRNA LOY said:

Let's be clear about one thing. Congress has a right to investigate, *to make laws*. But we question the right of any official to abuse citizens in order to make headlines. We question the right of Congress to ask any man what he thinks on political issues. We believe that the First Amendment forbids any legislation in the very field in which this Committee is acting. We think a lot of our freedom. We've become accustomed to it, but it was a brand new idea when Thomas Jefferson and James Madison and Benjamin Franklin wrote it in our Constitution. The other idea—the Un-American Committee's idea—is as old as history.

FRANK SINATRA said:

Once they get the movies throttled, how long will it be before the Committee goes to work on freedom of the air? How long will it be before we're told what we can and cannot say into a radio microphone? If you make a pitch on a nation-wide network for a square deal for the underdog, will they call you a Commie? Will we have to think Mr. Rankin's way to get in the elevator at Radio City? Are they gonna scare us into silence? I wonder.

EDWARD G. ROBINSON said:

It has been broadly suggested that Hollywood pictures are un-American when they make a villian of a landlord, a banker or a man with a fancy vest. Well, long before people were being slandered by being called Communists, William S. Hart was galloping across a movie screen like a ball of fire to pay off the mortgage on the old homestead. And the villian was the town banker, or a reasonable facsimile, the old scoundrel! By this definition, *East Lynne* was subversive propaganda; and the American kids who cheered all that hard riding in the sixth reel were wickedly undermined and they all grew up to be criminals, anarchists and overthrowers-of-the-government-by-force. BANG! BANG!

ROBERT YOUNG said:

The Thomas-Rankin Committee is not a new idea. It goes back for centuries. There was a similar committee on Un-Italian activities which subpoenaed Galileo, and a committee on Un-French activities which subpoenaed Joan of Arc. And a committee on Un-New England activities, three hundred years ago, which burned old women in a witch hunt at Salem, and hounded Roger Williams for saying, *I plead the cause of truth and innocence against the bloody doctrine of persecution for cause of conscience.*

Out of 2,000 years of men fighting and dying to think free, came an idea of justice; came a document called the Bill of Rights.

HELEN GAHAGAN DOUGLAS said:

As a member of the House of Representatives, I have consistently voted to abolish the Committee on Un-American Activities, because

I believe that the Committee as set up cannot avoid violating our guaranteed liberties.

WILLIAM WYLER said:

I wouldn't be allowed to make *The Best Years of Our Lives* in Hollywood today.

That is directly the result of the activities of the Un-American Activities Committee.

They are making decent people afraid to express their opinions. They are creating fear in Hollywood. Fear will result in self-censorship. Self-censorship will paralyze the screen.

In the last analysis, you will suffer. You will be deprived of entertainment which stimulates you, and you will be given a diet of pictures which conform to arbitrary standards of Americanism. I hope to make many more pictures as popular, as meaningful and as successful at the box office as *The Best Years of Our Lives*.

MELVYN DOUGLAS said:

Even members of Congress have denounced the Committee. Representative Adolph Sabath, Chairman of the House Rules Committee, said:

In all my Congressional experience of thirty-two years, I know of no committee so broadly condemned because of its conduct by people in all stages of life, and from all parts of the nation.

ARCHIBALD McLEISH said:

No issue was ever clearer than the issue the Thomas Committee has tossed into the faces of the American people. The most American of all American rights is the right of any man to think as he pleases and to say what he thinks. That right is protected against Congressional interference by the American Constitution. The question before the country is—can a Committee of Congress go indirectly by inquisition into a man's beliefs, what the Constitution forbids Congress to do directly: And if it can, what is left of the Constitution and the freedom it protects?

JOSEPH COTTEN said:

How often do you go to the movies? Once a week? Chances are you have probably seen *Pride of the Marines*. And do you remember *Objective Burma, Kitty Foyle,* and *Thirty Seconds Over Tokyo?* And such great classics as *All Quiet on the Western Front?* Actors, directors, writers and producers who gave you those pictures have been attacked and smeared as Un-American for putting subversive propaganda into their pictures.

GENE KELLY said:

The House Un-American Committee has called on the carpet some of the people who have been making your favorite movies. Did you happen to see *The Best Years of Our Lives,* the picture that won seven Academy Awards? Did you like it? Were you subverted by it? Did it make you Un-American? Did you come out of the movie with the desire to overthrow the government?

THE SCREEN WRITERS' GUILD and THE SCREEN DIRECTORS' GUILD said, in a resolution:

As Americans, devoted to our country and to the Constitution, which is its spiritual shape and form, we hereby resolve to defend the reputation of the industry in which we work against attack by the House Committee on Un-American Activities, whose chosen weapon is the cowardly one of inference, and whose apparent aim is to silence opposition to their extremist views, in the free medium of the motion pictures.

CLIFTON FADIMAN said:

The inquisitors of the Washington hearings would—if it had been within their power, or if they had ever heard of these men—called before their bar of slander such giants as these: Sinclair Lewis, for having written *Main Street:* Frank Norris, for having written *The Octopus:* Theodore Dreiser, *An American Tragedy:* Stephen Crane, for his attack on war in *The Red Badge of Courage:* Tolstoy, for *War and Peace:* Mark Twain, Shakespeare, Zola, Ibsen, Goethe, and a thousand others—all of them unfriendly witnesses, Mr. Thomas!

THE LOS ANGELES NEWSPAPER GUILD in a Resolution said:

The fear campaign among Hollywood studio employers, incited by the actions of the Thomas Committee and the threat of Federal censorship of the screen, induced and sponsored by William Randolph Hearst, is already prompting frightened and reactionary employers in other industries, newspaper plants and publishing houses to adopt the blacklist program aimed at liberal workers by the Association of Motion Picture Producers.

MARGARET SULLAVAN said:

Do you remember your school teacher reading these words: *Congress shall make no law respecting the establishment of religion, or prohibiting the free exercise thereof, or abridge the freedom of speech or of the press. . . .*

There's no double talk there; the intent is clear—the pattern defined—the meaning unclouded with doubt.

RICHARD CONTE said:

It wouldn't be fair just to quote the people who do not like the Committee. We believe in free speech, and in presenting both sides of the question. So we looked up some of the Committee's real friends. Here they are:

William Dudley Pelley said, *I founded the Silver Legion to propagandize the same principles that the Committee are now engaged in prosecuting.*

[223]

And who is William Dudley Pelley? He organized a Nazi-like gang called The Silver Shirts.

PAUL HENREID said:

I have the highest respect for the Committee and sympathize with its program.

This was said by Sylvester Viereck, convicted Nazi agent. And here's another quote:

I am in favor of the committee to be appointed again, and wish them to get more money.

That was said by Fritz Kuhn, German-American Bund leader, who was later jailed and deported.

FLORENCE ELDRIDGE said:

Here are some names that have been dragged into these hearings: Mr. Justice Murphy of the Supreme Court, Mrs. Franklin D. Roosevelt, Ambassador Joseph E. Davies, William Allen White, Dean Acheson, college presidents, judges, writers, historians, ministers and priests. The moving picture people who are being slandered today are in pretty good company.

EVELYN KEYES said:

James Colescott said, *The Un-American Committee program so closely parallels the program of the Klan that there is no distinguishable difference between them!*

And who is James Colescott? The Imperial Wizard of the Ku Klux Klan.

JOHN BEAL said:

There is not a court in the land where even a man suspected of murder cannot have his attorney rise to say "I object." And, yet, in

[224]

the Un-American Committee's hearings room in Washington, the lawyer who said "I object," was forcibly removed from the hearing.

VAN HEFLIN said:

The Bill of Rights is part of a long heritage of justice. A heritage which gives you the right to speak your mind without fear—which gives an accused man the right to answer his accusers: the right to be protected from slander and misstatements of fact. In no court in this land, is action taken on the basis of hearsay or personal opinion.

HAROLD E. STASSEN said:

We must not have governmental censorship of the screen, of radio, of books or of the press or the theatre. The day we seek to block the expression of dissent, the voice of opposition, in America, that day we lose something fundamental in the future well-being and strength of the American people.

JUNE HAVOC said:

You know, we're not experts on politics. We've been taking American freedom for granted, and not worrying about somebody taking it away from us. So we've had to ask questions to get the facts. Who is judging us? Who makes charges about our pictures degrading America? Who is the House Committee on Un-American Activities?

PAULETTE GODDARD said:

There is not a court in America which will admit questions that put words or opinions into the mouths of witnesses, or that indicate exactly what answer is wanted. Yet members of the Un-American Committee have repeatedly done this in the examination of witnesses. Time after time, they have asked questions which began "Is this what you mean to say?" Or—"Does this sum up your feelings?" Or—"In other words, you would say that . . . ?"

In spite of this handy technique of putting words into the mouths of witnesses—to this day no one has been able to point to any character, any scene, or any line from any picture which can be understood to advocate the overthrow of our government.

THE TEN
WHO WERE INDICTED

ALVAH BESSIE. Author of: *Swell in the Wilderness; Men in Battle; Bread and a Stone.*

Author of the following screenplays: *Northern Pursuit; The Very Thought of You; Objective Burma* (Original Story); *Hotel Berlin; Smart Woman.*

Received Guggenheim fellowship in creative writing in 1935.

HERBERT BIBERMAN. Directed the following movies: *One Way Ticket; Meet Nero Wolfe; The Master Race.* Wrote the following screen plays: *Revenge at Night; Prison Farm; Together Again; Action in Arabia; The Master Race.* Associate producer of *Abilene Town.* Wrote original story and was associate producer of *New Orleans.*

Mr. Biberman came to Hollywood from the Theater Guild of New York in 1935 under contract to Columbia Pictures as a director.

LESTER COLE. Author of the following screenplays: *None Shall Escape; Blood on the Sun; Fiesta; Romance of Rosy Ridge; Objective Burma* (co-author); *High Wall* (just released and starring, of all people, Robert Taylor).

EDWARD DMYTRYK. Director of the following movies: *Television Spy; Emergency Squad; Golden Gloves; Mystery Sea Raider; Her First Romance; The Devil Commands; Under Age; Sweetheart of the Campus; The Blonde from Singapore; Confessions of Boston Blackie; Lone Wolf in London; Seven Miles from Alcatraz; Hitler's Children; Captive Wild Woman; Behind the Rising Sun; Tender Comrade; Murder My Sweet; Back to Bataan; Cornered; Till the End of Time; So Well Remembered; Crossfire.*

RING LARDNER, JR. Author of the following screenplays: *Woman of the Year* (Motion Picture Academy Award for Best Original Screenplay 1942—collaboration with Michael Kanin); *The Cross of Lorraine; Tomorrow the World; Cloak and Dagger; Forever Amber* (collaboration with Philip Dunne).

Member, Executive Board Screen Writers Guild, several times since 1937.

JOHN HOWARD LAWSON. Author of the following plays: *Roger Bloomer; Processional; Nirvana; Loudspeaker; The International; Success Story; Gentlewoman; The Pure in Heart; Marching Song.* Also author of *Theory and Technique of Playwriting.*

Author of the following screenplays: *Blockade; Algiers; They Shall Have Music; Earthbound; Four Sons; Action in the North Atlantic; Sahara; Counterattack; Smashup.*

First president of Screenwriters Guild when it was organized in 1933.

ALBERT MALTZ. Author of: *The Cross and the Arrow* (a novel; special edition of 140,000 copies published by the Armed Services Editions for American servicemen); *The Underground Stream* (a novel); *Merry-Go-Round* (a play); *Peace on Earth* (a play); *Black Pit* (a play); *The Way Things Are* and other short stories. Winner of the 1938 O'Henry Memorial Award for the best American short story. Stories reprinted in Best Short Stories of 1936, 1939, 1941.

Author of the following screenplays: *This Gun for Hire; Destination Tokyo* (made an official training film by the U.S. Navy); *Pride of the Marines; Cloak and Dagger; Moscow Strikes Back* (English Commentary. Special award for the best foreign war documentary of 1942 from the Academy of Motion Picture Arts and Sciences. Selected best war documentary of 1942 by N.Y. Film Critics); *The House I Live In* (special award from Motion Picture Academy of Arts and Sciences, 1945); *The Naked City* (in collaboration with Malvin Wald).

Member of Authors League since 1932, variously on Authors League Council and Authors Guild Council. Member of Panel of Arbiters of the American Arbitration Association. Member of Executive Board of the Theatre Union 1933-37. Member Editorial Board of *Equality Magazine,* 1939-40. Instructor of Playwriting at the School of Adult Education, New York University, 1937-41. Instructor of Playwriting at the Writers Conference in the Rocky Mountains, 1939, '40.

SAMUEL ORNITZ. Author of: *Haunch, Paunch, & Jowl; Yankee Passional; Round the World with Jocko the Great.*

Author of the following screenplays: *The Man Who Reclaimed His Head; Three Kids and a Queen; Two Wise Maids; Three Faces West.*

ADRIAN SCOTT. Author of the following screenplays: *Mr. Lucky; Miss Suzie Slagle; Parson of Panamint; Keeping Company.* Producer of the following movies: *Murder My Sweet; My Pal Wolf; Cornered; Deadline at Dawn; Crossfire; So Well Remembered* (produced in England); *The Boy with the Green Hair; Mr. Lincoln's Whiskers.*

DALTON TRUMBO. Author of: *Eclipse* (a novel); *Washington Jitters* (a novel; dramatized version presented by Theatre Guild); *Johnny Got His Gun* (National Booksellers Association plaque as Most Original Novel of 1939); *The Remarkable Andrew* (a novel).

Wrote short stories, essays and poetry for: *The Saturday Evening Post; Liberty Magazine; McCalls Magazine; The Forum; Vanity Fair; North American Review; New Masses; Script Magazine; Mainstream Magazine.*

Author of the following screenplays: *A Man to Remember* (chosen among Ten Best of 1938); *Kitty Foyle* (screenplay nominated for Academy Award); *A Guy Named Joe* (Boxoffice Magazine Award); *Thirty Seconds over Tokyo* (Boxoffice Magazine Award; Parents Magazine Medal picture; Best Ten of Year: Gallup Poll); *Our Vines Have Tender Grapes* (Boxoffice Magazine Award; Parents Magazine Medal picture); also a dozen other films, including *Tender Comrade, Five Came Back; The Remarkable Andrew*, etc.

Former director, Screen Writers Guild. Founding editor, *The Screen Writer*, official publication Screen Writers Guild. Member Editorial Board, *Mainstream Magazine.* Chairman, Writers for Roosevelt, 1944. U.S. Accredited War Correspondent, Luzon, Okinawa, Balikpapen, Dutch Borneo, summer 1945.